FOUND IN CHRISTM *...TREE AFTER*
YEAR'S EVE DRINK

ner
ses to
gh field
he sees
t

DUBLIN AND
CORK GET JOBS,
WHILE NAVAN
GETS SILAGE

WHO'S
IN THE
COFFIN

S JOB BY MYSELF', SAYS CORK PENSIONER

A dung deal at Ardfert
art exhibition

**Stop
the
lights
and get
stoned**

N DRINKS PINT IN
URT — JUDGE CALLS
M TO THE BAR

*Longford
snubbed by
Google Maps*

MAN TRIED TO
VIBRATORS
SEX SHOP

**POTHOLES SO BAD ASTRONAUTS
COULD TRAIN IN THEM**

gets overdue
ck – 58 years late

Woman fined
for driving with
onion ring

METER
IDN'T
RKING

MEDIUM-SIZED TOWN, FAIRLY BIG STORY

THE STORIES THAT MADE THE

HEADLINES IN IRELAND'S LOCAL NEWSPAPERS ...

AND NOWHERE ELSE

The Author

Currently a fixture on TV3's 'Ireland AM' show, Ronan Casey brings the most ludicrous stories from Ireland's local newspapers to air every Friday morning. Perhaps Ireland's only local newspaper addict, he also presented a successful newspaper review for RTÉ 2FM. A widely-experienced broadcaster and journalist, he has written for many national newspapers and has spent over a decade on the frontlines with some of Ireland's best-known local newspapers. He is the author of the critically acclaimed, bestselling biography of the late Joe Dolan for Penguin in 2008.

He lives in Mullingar where his wife and two children have evicted him to the garage to indulge his newspaper habit.

MEDIUM SIZED TOWN | FAIRLY BIG STORY

* * * RONAN CASEY * * *

THE STORIES THAT MADE THE HEADLINES IN
IRELAND'S LOCAL NEWSPAPERS ... AND NOWHERE ELSE

GILL & MACMILLAN

Gill & Macmillan
Hume Avenue, Park West, Dublin 12
www.gillmacmillanbooks.ie

Selection © Ronan Casey 2014
978 07171 62017

Artwork by Fuchsia MacAree
Design and print origination by www.grahamthew.com
Printed and bound by CPI Group (UK) Ltd, CR0 4YY

The paper used in this book comes from the wood pulp of managed
forests. For every tree felled, at least one tree is planted, thereby
renewing natural resources.

A CIP catalogue record for this book is available from the
British Library.

13542

For Deirdre, who said yes

And James and Emily, the rays of light

and love that followed

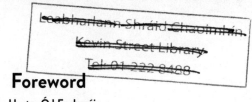
Foreword

by Hector Ó hEochagáin

MEDIUM-SIZED TOWN, FAIRLY BIG STORY is a window to the soul of the country. It is a snapshot of the way we were, the way we are, and – please God – the way we'll always be. These stories in Ronan's book show the humour, personality, character and wit of the country and its people in a way I've never read before.

Where else in the world has a local newspaper system quite like Ireland? Wherever you live, in whichever town you dwell, there is always a day when the local paper is plopped onto the kitchen table. For me, it was the *Meath Chronicle* of a Thursday in Navan. I always checked the sport, the court, and who was playing in the local nightclub at the weekend.

Personally, 'Medium-Sized Town, Fairly Big Story' was one of the cornerstones of my very successful 'Breakfast with Hector' radio show on RTÉ 2FM. The audience knew the slot, they waited for the slot and they reacted to the slot every week. It put a smile on their faces and made a lot of people laugh on their early-morning commute all around the country.

Ronan did a brilliant job bringing local news to the nation on the radio; he continues to do so on television with 'Ireland AM' on TV3, and, most importantly, in this fine book.

We have lost a fair bit in this country, we've changed a lot in this country, but – fingers crossed – our local newspapers will remain intact for future generations.

As the song went:

'I live in a quiet town, where nothing ever happens,
There's never any gossip to keep the nosy people chatting,
But once in a while some news comes around that doesn't really bore me,
Medium-Sized Town, Fairly Big Story ...'

Meas mór,

Hector

Preface

THIS BOOK IS A celebration of Ireland's regional newspapers and the wild and wonderful tales they publish with a straight face every single week. Over 1.5 million Irish people read a local paper every week, and from an exceedingly young age I was one of them.

When I was growing up, our house was full of papers. My father bought more papers every day than most people do in a week. Every evening we'd fight over who got to read Con Houlihan first, and on a Sunday you wouldn't be able to see the carpet, such was the number of papers on the floor, but on a Wednesday peace reigned, as we had a local paper each.

There were two local papers printed in Mullingar: the *Topic* and the *Examiner*. Like all local papers, they were best known by their abbreviated names. You only added the county name to them if you were talking about them outside the county. As a youngster I often stood outside the back door of their respective 'works' to watch, hear and smell them roll off the presses. It was a strange attraction which, I'm afraid to admit, has lasted a lifetime.

When I was anywhere in Ireland, be it holidays, festivals, adventures or visiting relations, one of the first things I looked for was a local paper. When I was a student in Dublin, my contemporaries all tried to be intelligent with their *Irish Times* and their *Guardian* whilst I would rock in with a copy of the *Kerryman* or *Kerry's Eye* under my arm. Bar holidays in Killarney as a nipper, I had absolutely no link to Kerry whatsoever. They, like so many other titles, were enjoyable reads. For a few years, the regional-paper section in Eason's in O'Connell Street was the best library in Dublin. Every week I'd choose a different one. On the dole in Galway years later, I always found a few quid for a local rag.

As the years passed and with no shaking off of this disease, the only cure was to go and work for an actual newspaper. I've been very lucky to have written for quite a few of them since 2000, both national and local. Having secured a radio slot (and then a TV slot) bringing stories from the local papers to a national audience, I've somehow ended up reading them for a living; talk about the dream job!

However, there is a downside. My house is now full of newspapers. My shed is full of newspapers. My head was full of stories from these newspapers.

In selecting stories for this book, I would like to think the people I have 'regaled' with such yarns played a part, for it was family and friends who encouraged me to put them into book form. Thinking back, I imagine their motive was probably so they would never hear me tell them the stories again ... But these stories are important; they are the lifeblood of local papers and local communities. They may not make a splash nationally, but in the Medium-Sized Towns from which they came, they are the Fairly Big Story!

Longford couple find spider with 'Sacred Heart' markings

A TEGENARIA, OR giant house spider, which bears an apparent likeness to Jesus Christ, has appeared at a house in Longford. Edel Sweeney found the spider in her home and noticed the markings on the spider's back closely resemble the iconic image of the Sacred Heart. Edel's boyfriend captured the harmless spider in his hands before taking some photographs. The story was covered by the *Sunday World*.

MAN WAS 'SICK AS A DOG' AFTER DRINKING POITÍN MEANT FOR SICK DOG

A MAN WAS RUSHED to Mayo General Hospital after he drank some poitín which was meant for a sick dog. The man appeared before Castlebar District Court after he was arrested for intoxication in a public place and for threatening and abusive behaviour in the A&E Department of Mayo General Hospital.

He told the court he drank the illegal alcohol in his home in Crossmolina and that he could not remember anything after drinking it. He was transferred to Mayo General Hospital, but the ambulance personnel would only bring him if they were accompanied by four Gardaí for safety reasons.

The man said he was 'totally ashamed' of what happened and explained that he did not know it was poitín he was drinking at the time, as it was in a clear bottle. 'I didn't know what I was drinking at the time. I was brought by two ambulance men, but I don't remember anything after that. It is a blank,' he told the court.

He explained he later discovered the drink was for a sick dog, and when he was asked by Judge Mary Devins if he rubbed it into the dog, he replied, 'The dog wasn't drunk, he doesn't drink it.' The matter was met with laughter in the court and defending solicitor Peter Loftus said his client had a serious reaction to the poitín.

Garda Brett told the court that after the incident the defendant was co-operative and was not aggressive to the Gardaí. He said he apologised when he was sober and added that that does not always happen. Judge Devins said if the man wrote a letter to the A&E staff apologising to the hospital staff and donated €300 to the Ann Sullivan Centre for the Deaf and Blind she would give him the benefit of the Probation Act.

GARY'S GLEE AT

RETURN OF HIS

COMMUNION MONEY

A WEXFORD BOY who lost his First Communion money on the street was overjoyed after the cash was handed back by kind-hearted restaurant staff. Gary O'Sullivan (8) of Whiterock Hill was in tears after losing his wallet containing €260 during a shopping trip with his mother Colleen the day after making his first Communion.

It was picked up by Anna Gorska, a member of staff at Cappuchino's, the day before she was due to go home to Poland on holidays, and not knowing who owned it, she locked it away safe and sound. A colleague reading the *Wexford People* learned about Gary's disappointment and – just in time to make the paper – Gary was reunited with his Communion cash. To show his appreciation, he immediately went out and bought the girls a great big bunch of flowers. 'He's thrilled to bits,' his mother said upon return of the wallet.

Limerick parking signs changed to read 'Red Light District'

AN ONGOING ISSUE in Limerick city centre has been highlighted in a novel way after an unknown person – or persons – changed traffic signs on Catherine Street to read 'Red Light District' on Monday. Gardaí have been informed of an attempt to interfere with regulatory traffic signs in the city centre in a case which has mystified local authorities.

Three traffic signs in total, on the junctions of Roches, Cecil and Glentworth streets with Catherine Street, were overlaid with a sticker, cleverly designed to mimic the underlying traffic signs and reading 'Red Light District, in effect by order Luan–Sath 18.00pm to/go 04.00am Mon–Sat'.

A member of the public notified the *Leader* to the matter early on Monday morning, which has perplexed city council officials, and as a criminal offence, it has been reported to Gardaí. The stickers were removed almost immediately after city council were informed by this newspaper. Traffic Engineer Rory McDermott said he had 'never seen anything like this before'.

'We would get lots of interference with signs, but never anything like that,' he explained. 'We get street names' plates stolen, around the colleges and universities we get warning signs stolen, bollards are stolen, but this is very specific. Is there some kind of activity going on up there that someone is trying to bring to the attention of? It is very clever. I will talk to the police about it. It is interference with a regulatory sign, it is a criminal offence,' he added.

Within half an hour of this newspaper reporting the signs having been interfered with, they had been removed by council officials and the Gardaí informed.

'I DID COUNCIL'S JOB BY MYSELF', SAYS CORK PENSIONER

A PENSIONER GOT so tired of waiting for the council to fix a rancid broken pipe that she ended up doing the work herself, digging a couple of feet into the ground to do the work of trained professionals. Margarita Adair had waited five months for them to come and fix a broken pipe outside her Kiskeam home, which had been leaking fetid, stinking water for months – and she'd simply had enough. The Kiskeam woman got out her shovel and tackled the backbreaking work herself.

Sixty-six-year-old Margarita is the sole carer of her 82-year-old husband, David, who is terminally ill with lung cancer. She told the *Corkman* how she first visited the county council offices in Newmarket on 5 December 2011 to ask them to send someone to fix a pipe which they themselves had put in many years ago and which had become blocked.

'The stagnant water was backed up really high at the back of our house,' Margarita explained. 'It was getting blacker and more foul-smelling each day, along with attracting insects of all sorts.

'This in itself is bad enough, but with my husband's lung cancer it is the last thing we need to have a source of infection just outside the door, let alone have the house flooded, which was a real threat in those months when it rained incessantly.

'I went time and again', she continued, 'and the nice clerk man said – amazed every time he saw me – "they haven't been?", and wrote it down again in the book.'

After waiting five months and nine days, she decided she could stand it no longer and started doing the job herself. 'It is not only very hard work for a 66-year-old-woman but also extremely dangerous, as I could very well hurt myself and then what would my husband do without me? Every evening after digging, I feel like I have been run over by a truck.'

The ultimate irony from Margarita and David's point of view is that in the past 17 years since they have been living in Kiskeam, they have fully paid all their taxes, and just recently paid the controversial household charge in the very office where Margarita 'has gone so many times to beg to get the job done'.

Having contacted the *Corkman* on Monday, Margarita informed staff at the local council office of her intention and was told that an official had, in fact, already called to the house. However, Margarita and David say they saw no one from the council and received no letter and no phone calls.

On Monday afternoon, a council representative finally called to the house promising that repairs would be undertaken and Margarita was able to confirm that council workers were on the job outside her home as this paper was going to press on Wednesday.

CRAFTY OFFALIAN SELLING MONEY FOR MORE THAN ITS CURRENT VALUE ON EBAY

IF YOU WEREN'T SURE how crafty Offaly people are, this should give you an idea! An enterprising Offalian has seemingly bypassed selling products or services to make money and has opted to sell money itself for more than its stated value instead!

A private seller based in Offaly has offered up a new Irish €5 note for sale on eBay. The seller is willing to ship the glossy new note anywhere in the world, but potential buyers will have to stump up €2.25 on top of the sale price for postage. Currently bids for the €5 note have reached €6.90 but could go higher as the sale will continue for another hour or so. The seller is also selling nine British pennies and five Roman coins, as well as a host of other monies.

NO CLEAN GETAWAY IN POWER-WASHER THEFT

Ballinrobe bullock's a mammy's boy

HERD OF BULLINROBE'S new traffic system? As famous as Ballinrobe is for its twice-weekly livestock sale at the town's mart, it is becoming equally famous for rebel livestock wandering the streets. On Wednesday last a lone Charolais bullock had escaped the confines of Ballinrobe Mart on the Claremorris road at around 1 p.m. The bullock, which was destined for sale later that day, had made a break for it and run up Watson's Lane – followed on foot by its owner, Freddie Yarnell.

Speaking to the *Mayo News*, Mr Yarnell said the animal took a right up Glebe Street, before pausing at the old courthouse for a time and then running the wrong way up the one-way Main Street, startling pedestrians and drivers alike. 'He was like Shergar, and I was like Usain Bolt,' joked Mr Yarnell in his Brummie accent. 'Everybody was just pointing as I passed, knowing well what I was looking for,' he laughed. Eye witness Ray McGreal told the *Mayo News* that he saw the bullock run past shops, cars and people. 'He mustn't have wanted to be sold, or else he was on his way to Jennings' Abattoir for an early slaughter!' he joked.

Mr Yarnell finally located the bullock in a field just off Bowgate Street in the town. However, the animal was not about to give up his freedom easily and he crossed the Bulkan River. Thinking on his feet, Yarnell returned to his own land and brought the bullock's mother in a trailer to the field in the hope that the rogue bullock would 'listen to mammy'. 'She gave one bleep and he came like a thunderbolt,' Mr Yarnell enthused. After a three-and-a-half-hour chase, Yarnell transported the rogue bullock to the mart for a 5 p.m. sale.

'I got him back to the mart at 4.40 p.m. and into the ring, and the guys went mad bidding for him. €1,000 for a mighty animal. When I think of all the damage he could have done ... but he was a pure gentleman and never hurt anyone,' he said thankfully.

This is the second time the town has experienced a bovine shopper. In 2009 a bull hit the headlines when it popped into Cummins' Supervalu (not a china shop) to 'have a look around'. Bruno the Bull was caught on CCTV entering the supermarket and running riot through the aisles, with his hapless owner chasing after him. Miraculously, nobody was hurt in that incident either and the bull was eventually recaptured.

One thing's for sure in Ballinrobe, their beef is fresh and 100 per cent traceable.

SNAKES IN THE BED

A quiet neighbourhood in Mountrath was somewhat rattled recently when a woman discovered a three-and-a-half-foot snake under her bed. Margaret O'Brien, of Fr O'Connor Crescent, bent down to pick up what she thought was a children's toy sticking out from under the bed, but she got the fright of her life when the orange and brown striped tail suddenly moved. 'She thought it was a kid's toy, like the tail of a Tigger teddy bear, but when she bent down to pick it up it disappeared under the bed. It was a big fright,' said her son Michael.

Understandably shaken, Margaret rang both Michael and her daughter's boyfriend. The lads managed to bag the snake with the use of a long poker, then they called the Gardaí; although the guards admitted they weren't sure what to do with the reptile and they suggested waiting until morning before bringing it to a pet shop.

'Someone said there was a vacant house nearby where there were pet snakes, so the letting agent came down and went in,' Michael continued. 'The fellow who lived there had left and there were three or four snakes in the house and some terrapins. The house wasn't in great condition,' he added.

The snakes were being kept in a glass box, but a door had been left open and the slithery escapee managed to make its way up to the O'Brien household. Having bagged the snake, the men returned it to the glass box and waited for the Gardaí and the ISPCA to arrive. Eventually the man renting the house returned and collected the animals. It is understood he was in the process of moving house and had been absent from the premises for a couple of weeks. While there was obvious concern among local residents, Conor Dowling, chief inspector with the ISPCA, said the snake was not dangerous and there were no animal welfare issues with the property.

'It was a corn snake. It could give you a bite, but there would be no real damage,' Mr Dowling said, adding that other breeds present in the house were a California kingsnake and a ball python. He explained that the terrapins were removed from the property and brought somewhere more suitable, but the snakes remain with their owner.

DOGS IN MOUNTMELLICK MAY SOON BE IN NAPPIES

DOGS IN MOUNTMELLICK may soon be going around wearing nappies. That was one of the suggestions made at the recent Joint Policing Committee (JPC) meeting in the town on the ongoing debate on the problem of dog fouling. Town councillors have been raising the issue at every possible opportunity in an attempt to have the matter sorted out. At their last town council meeting, they admitted to talking about the issue for the past three years with absolutely no success. This resulted in an equally memorable headline in the same paper a few weeks previously: 'Councillors agree they've been talking crap for years ...'

They again took another opportunity to highlight the issue at the JPC meeting. Councillor Bobby Delaney was first out of the traps when he asked Superintendent Philip Lyons what powers Gardaí have in addressing the issue. Councillor Delaney said: 'A person came to me and wanted to know had dog walkers got licences for their dogs and would the Gardaí step in when they see dogs fouling?'

Superintendent Lyons said that all dog owners must have licences and be responsible for them. He said: 'We don't take action if a dog fouls a footpath. It is possible to approach people who are walking dogs to ask them to produce a licence for their dog. But there is no law against people walking dogs on footpaths.'

Councillor Denis O'Mara said the problem of dog litter is so bad in the town that 'you can't walk on the footpaths anymore'. Councillor Delaney said: 'What I'd like to see is that if the Gardaí see it going on that they can do something.' Councillor Paddy Buggy quipped: 'We'll soon have to get nappies for the dogs,' a comment which was given serious concern. Superintendent Lyon finished by saying, 'Leave it with me and I'll look into it.'

'How many council staff does it take to fix a leaky pipe?'

HOW MANY COUNCIL WORKERS does it take to fix a pipe? That was the question asked when a water break brought Macroom to a standstill on a Friday afternoon in July. The town experienced tailbacks in both directions of the main N22 road as a number of council staff attempted to fix the pipe.

The issue was raised by Councillor Ted Lucey (FG) at Tuesday night's meeting of the local town council. While Councillor Lucey was at pains to emphasise that he had no problem with the council workers, management's deployment of staff was not spared his ire. 'I was down at the butcher's last Friday at 3 p.m. and looking out the window I saw three men directing traffic, one man in a JCB, two down the hole with the pipe and nine more up on the path looking down the hole.

'I was embarrassed to be in the butcher's looking out the window at nine men looking down a hole. If it was open heart surgery, there wouldn't be so many in the theatre. It was the talk of the town over the weekend,' he said. Councillor Lucey said that while the trio charged with directing traffic were effective, he did not know why so many staff were needed during the daytime for such a job.

'I counted them all, all council staff. I can't see why that can't be done at night. If we pay 15 people to do it during the day, then surely we can afford to pay a half dozen to do it at night. I have nothing against the staff, they're doing what they're told. But it was appalling management,' he said.

Town engineer Damien Murphy said that the management of water services was under the remit of the county council's area engineer.

Hole for sale in Longford

AN ADVERTISEMENT HAS APPEARED on DoneDeal selling a hole in County Longford. While it does not specify exactly where the hole is, it does state that it can be transferred to a new home. It is described as 'Big hole for sale. A real fine hole it is'. The hole is priced at €1,000,000 and the seller invites 'all txts, private numbers, hole kickers or time wasters' to view the hole. There is also a photograph of a shovel in the hole; however, it is not clear at this time if the shovel is part of the deal.

ALL THAT GLISTENS ISN'T GOLD

A FERMANAGH MAN who tried to turn his own faeces into gold by putting it on an electric heater has been jailed for three months. The bizarre experiment caused around £3,000 worth of damage to his Housing Executive home in a block of flats in Enniskillen in July.

The man admitted to arson and endangering the lives of others. His Honour Judge McFarland told him, 'Rather bizarrely you were attempting to make gold from human faeces and waste products.

'It was an interesting experiment to fulfil the alchemist's dream but wasn't going to succeed,' stated the Judge.

COUNCIL CANNOT THINK OF ANYTHING

EIGHT OF THE NINE-MAN strong Kilkee Town Council couldn't manage to think of a single motion between them in advance of Monday's meeting. Shockingly, this was a repeat of what happened at the January meeting when they couldn't think of anything to talk about either.

The only councillor who managed to place a motion on the agenda during the April meeting, and in January, was Councillor Claire Haugh. One of her three motions on Monday proposed that Kilkee Town Council along with other councils establish a cross-party working group to oppose any Government move to get rid of town councils!

'I think it's important that our own town council here in Kilkee is retained,' Councillor Haugh said. 'We should make a lot more noise about it. We are the voice of the town.' Councillor Paddy Collins said the nine town councillors are superb value for money. 'We're only costing the State €3 a day,' he revealed.

Other items that made the agenda, prepared by Kilkee town clerk John Corry for Monday's meeting, included updates on the Cliff Walk, a presentation from Clare ISPCA dog warden Frankie Coote, the Kilkee beach lighting project and a presentation to fifth- and sixth-class pupils from Scoil Réalt na Mara.

TOP PRINCE WILLIAM LOOKALIKE IS AN ATHLONE TRAVELLER

THE TOP PRINCE WILLIAM lookalike, currently working in the UK, is an Athlone man. Marc Rhattigan is busier than ever due to his uncanny resemblance to the soon-to-be-married Prince. The 28-year-old is proud of his roots. 'I am very proud of my Irish traveller roots and I would not swap them for the world. My dad's side of the family still live on sites and they are amazing people. I've never actually lived on one but spent most of my time on them growing up.'

Currently working as a radiographer, his career as a lookalike began in 1997, when he was just 14, after he was mobbed by a crowd while on a day trip to London Zoo shortly after the death of Princess Diana.

THE MAN WITH 100 FAMILY MEMBERS

NORTH DUBLIN MAN Matthew 'Matt' Murphy has lots to celebrate after welcoming the 100th member of his family into the world, great-grandchild Alan Savage. Matt, from Man O'War, is 'over the moon' thanks to the arrival of baby Alan, to the delight of parents Keith and his partner Mandy. Keith is Matt's grandson and Alan is his 49th great-grandchild. The 85-year-old has eleven children of his own – seven sons Gerry, John, Matt Junior, Frank, Paddy, Tim and George, and four daughters Marie, Kathleen, Ann (grandmother of baby Alan) and Peg, as well as 38 grandchildren, 49 great-grandchildren and two great-great-grandchildren.

'He is absolutely delighted and can't believe this is the 100th addition to the family,' Matt's son Gerry told the *Fingal Independent*. 'We were counting it out and had to double-check that we had the numbers right because there are so many of us! It's a big landmark to reach, you would have to knock on a lot of doors to find someone who has a family of 100.

'He's just glad he doesn't have to buy Christmas presents for all his grandchildren and great-grandchildren,' Gerry laughed.

Almost all the family live close to Matt in the north County Dublin area, apart from daughter Peg and her family who are based in Wexford, so Matt is never short of visitors young and old. Matt will be 86 in February and there might be a big family get-together then to mark the occasion. Only problem is finding a venue big enough!

Originally from Wexford, Matt moved to Man O'War to take up a position on Nancy and Barry Cassin's farm, where he worked for decades and continues to visit on a regular basis. After his wife left, Matt reared his eleven children as a single father, working seven days a week to support them.

MOO-VING WITH THE TIMES – CLUB ENLISTS CASH COW TO RAISE FUNDS

A RARE SCOTTISH Highland 'Coo' who likes to go to the toilet will help a Limerick club raise funds for floodlights. Bruff GAA Club's luscious pitch, upon which Christy Ring once played, is usually traversed by agile hurlers and sprightly footballers, but on 28 August next the star player will be a rare Bonnie of Drumbar breed, whose bowel movements will be carefully observed by all.

In an effort to raise money for floodlights, the committee at Bruff GAA Club are dividing up their famous pitch into virtual squares and then taking bets on which square the Scottish cow will take a dump on. Supporters will be asked to buy tickets which will correlate to a square on the pitch. If the cow scutters on your square, then you stand to win a very fragrant €1,000 cash prize. They are calling the once-in-a-lifetime event the Cow Dung Drop, and they hope to raise €30,000, which will cover floodlights and an all-weather pitch. Tickets are €5 each or €20 for five.

Bonnie is one of only eight Scottish Highland 'Coos' in the country and her long coat means she never has to be housed in the wintertime. 'They would survive anywhere – even on a GAA pitch!' explained her owner Pat Hayes of Athlacca. Pat played hurling for Bruff up to senior level, and managed the footballers, and Bonnie has been living on his farm for the past six years. 'I always liked them – they are a cool animal' said Pat, who is also a teacher at Coláiste Chiaráin in Croom.

Ger Browner, chairman of Bruff GAA Club, says this is 'definitely a different and novel way of fundraising and the club finance committee are to be complimented on their endeavours and vision in seeing the requirement for this facility and now going about raising the finance'.

Macroom man wants to run cars on whiskey

Professor Martin Tangney, a University College Cork graduate, has developed a system to extract energy from the by-products of whiskey and convert it to biofuel which can go straight into engines without modification. Cars would not have to be converted in order to run on this fuel. BP has researched a blend of butanol and petrol, and is interested in the whiskey blend, so pretty soon it'll be OK to drink and drive.

Giant slugs are invading Dundalk footpaths & causing havoc

GIANT SLUGS ARE causing walkers, joggers and runners grief as they attempt to avoid killing the slimy creatures while out exercising. Paul Cumiskey, a runner, told the *Dundalk Democrat* this week that the slugs are 'giant creatures' and there is a 'sea' of them. 'I was running on the footpath near the Retail Park and the entrance to Bay Estate during the week and next of all I see all these slugs, they seemed to be coming from the bushes, there was so many of them. These weren't like normal slugs that I have ever seen before, a lot of them were quite big. I obviously didn't want to step on them and kill them so I was tip-toeing around them. ... Because there was so many of them, it was a sea of slugs, I decided to cross over to the other side of the road. The first thing I noticed was that there was slugs here as well and so many of them. I couldn't believe my eyes.'

Meanwhile, environmentalist and Green Party Councillor Mark Dearey said that he has come across 'four-inch slugs' and urged people not to kill the slimy invertebrates. 'Slugs are part of the food chain, they are valuable to the chain. We learn to live with them', he said. 'It's been a very wet summer and slugs are only active in the warm weather, so that's the reason why they are out. They can be quite big, I've come across four-inch slugs before. Everybody is complaining about the slugs.

'I would encourage people not to kill them. If they are pests in your garden, then use organic ways to get rid of them.'

MICKEY MOUSE IS A CAT

THIS IS NO MICKEY MOUSE STORY. It seems that the man who built a global empire on cartoon characters known to us all has Kilkenny connections.

From George Clooney to Barack Obama, Kilkenny connections have been well researched and now another famous figure – deceased yet arguably one of the most famous people of all time – has strong links to this county. The man who brought the world Mickey Mouse is, in fact, a cat. Galway genealogist, William Henry, recently traced Walt Disney's roots to Gowran, a town more famous for the animated crowds at the races than cartoons.

Kilkenny genealogist Pat Nolan said he was aware of persistent rumours that Walt Disney was descended from people around the Carlow-Kilkenny area. Mr Nolan said that pinpointing the townland where Walt Disney came from was another issue. 'There's an old story of two towns vying to claim Walt Disney's heritage. They called in a genealogist to trace the family.

After two months', study the genealogist had narrowed it down to six towns!' said Mr Nolan.

Walt Disney's great-grandfather Arundel Elias Disney was born in Kilkenny c.1801. In 1832 Arundel Elias married Maria Swan, who gave birth to their son Kepple Disney, Walt Disney's grandfather, on November 2 of the same year. The family ended up farming in Marceline, Missouri, where young Walt was born on 5 December 1901.

By the age of 16 Walt Disney was serving in the Red Cross as an ambulance driver during World War One. After the War, he stayed in Kansas and worked as an advertising cartoonist. He had much bigger ambitions, and in 1920 he created and marketed his first original animated cartoons. In 1923 Walt Disney left Kansas City with $40 in his pocket and set out for Hollywood. It was five years later when Disney's most famous character, Mickey Mouse, first appeared on screens, and the rest as they say is history ...

AWE AS 'VIRGIN MARY' APPEARS ON GRAIG' HILL

People are flocking to a County Kilkenny golf course after a 'revelation' – a clear image of the Virgin Mary with the infant Jesus in her arms – was suddenly discovered, despite being there for years.

Situated just two kilometres outside Graignamanagh near St Mullin's, rising high above the picturesque Carrigleade golf course are the Blackstairs Mountains. A bizarre formation in the rock, gravel and heather, with a scale in the hundreds of metres, is striking at a glance – and even more so when gazed upon for longer. It appears to depict the Madonna and Child.

'A couple of gentlemen playing golf pointed it out, and we instantly saw what they were talking about,' Bridie Galavan said, who with her husband Dan runs the course. 'Then another golfer here yesterday looked up at it and said he just couldn't believe it. It looks like Our Lady, and she's holding another figure, a head, and the way he sits it looks like a child.'

Already, many local people and those from further afield are making the 'pilgrimage' to see for themselves what the fuss is all about. Dubbed 'Our Lady of Carrigleade', it is fast becoming the talk of the town and indeed the rest of the county. What is most baffling is the fact that, until this week, the bizarre geological phenomenon was never spotted by anyone. It's almost as though it suddenly appeared overnight. 'We have never noticed it until now,' Bridie said. Her mother and sister have both made the journey up to see the image. 'And we'd have always been here. It's very strange.'

Some cynics have argued that the likeness is more akin to Mount Rushmore in the US, which depicts the heads of four American presidents, but for most who see it there is no mistaking the resemblance to Our Lady – or 'a lady' at the very least. The majority of supposed 'Marian Apparitions' are fleeting or vision-like, and 'sightings' of this nature, not least in terms of its size and location, are rare.

The stunning vista of the mountains, with the Blackstairs on one side and Brandon Hill on the other, already makes Carrigleade an aesthetically pleasing spot for golfers. Now many will be wondering if having Our Lady watching over them will have any bearing on their fortune over the 18 holes.

TIDY TOWNS
CLEANING UP
UNDER JUDGE

JUDGE SEAMUS HUGHES'S decision to make defendants pay for the upkeep of their town is beginning to mount up to a tidy sum: one day's takings from the District Court in Mullingar earlier this month topped the €1,200 mark! The Mullingar Tidy Towns Committee are delighted with the boost, and since the Judge took office earlier this summer, the town's Tidy Towns ranking has gone up.

Their chairman Brian Reidy admits to the paper that the committee has been a bit strapped of late, and he says it's better served on the streets than in the coffers of the Department of Justice. 'The people of Mullingar are going to get the money,' he says. 'We even had one fellow paying over his money to us saying he was delighted it was going to go to good use!' So, here is an example that crime does pay!

Colossal cabbage grown in Myshall!

FOR ANYONE WHO ever doubted they could be born under a head of cabbage ... just check out the colossal cabbages they grow in Myshall!

It seems like half the parish could be fed by Mary O'Toole, Shangarry, Myshall, thanks to an enormous head of cabbage, grown by her green-fingered daughter Marian.

The cabbage was planted in April this year, and with lots of loving care, along with a few slug pellets to keep the pests at bay, the cabbages absolutely blossomed, growing ten times the size of a normal head. 'There were a few of them big, but that was the biggest,' laughed Marian. 'It still hasn't been picked,' she added. Marian didn't exactly reveal the secret to getting her cabbages so big but joked that 'lots of talking to them and minding them helps'.

CAVAN'S OLDEST MAN REVEALS HIS SECRET

THE SECRET TO a long life is hard work and porridge. Michael Fitzsimmons was given the honorary title of 'Cavan's oldest man' by family and friends as he celebrated his 105th birthday. Mr Fitzsimmons, from Knockateggart, Stradone, was divulging a few tips on longevity as he enjoyed the day at the Lavey Inn, Cavan.

The secret is hard work, porridge, riding his bicycle until the age of 100 and not taking any holidays in the past 105 years, quipped the jovial birthday boy. 'He rode the bicycle all his life up until 100 ... then we had to let the wind out of the tyres,' his son Michael junior joked. 'He received the President's Bounty when he turned 100 and he was delighted with that.' Mr Fitzsimmons, who was a builder and renovator, turned 105 on Tuesday, 23 February. The party was held a few days later for 70 friends and family.

Titanic runs aground in Mullinasole

ONE HUNDRED YEARS after the 'greatest ship ever built' left the dry dock in Belfast and sailed into history, the *Titanic* is now casting its shadow over the shimmering waters of Donegal Bay. The Salmon Inn, at Mullinasole near Donegal Town, has become a fitting resting place for a 1/25th scale model of the RMS *Titanic*. It was built by local food writer Zack Gallagher, along with Jim Canavan and Gerald Drury from the St Francis National School Parents', Association, as the school's float in the Donegal town St Patrick's Day parade. It won the overall prize for best float on the day.

Now the *Titanic* (or rather half of the *Titanic*) now sits proudly in the garden of local publican and restaurateur Martin Quinn. 'We couldn't find anywhere to keep it and it was such a shame to let it go to ruin,' said Zack. 'An offer was made by some members of the local Credit Union to display it in their office window. A lovely gesture indeed, but we tried in vain to get it through the door,' he added. Martin Quinn, of the Salmon Inn, heard about the plight of the local boat-builders and came to their rescue.

A keen fisherman and sailor himself, he didn't want to see the ship sink so soon after its glorious maiden voyage. 'I've spent most of my life by the sea and I thought it would be a shame if the *Titanic* float couldn't, well, float!' said Martin. 'So, we have it in the garden for the moment as we are building a temporary floating pontoon for the boat to sit on. She'll look great sitting on the water, from the windows of the bar and restaurant, especially when the sun sinks behind her in the western sky.'

The model is only 'half a *Titanic*', as it was built to represent the great ship when it was sinking. 'I was going to build a full-length scale model,' Zack explains. 'But it was easier on the budget to give the impression that half of her is under the water.'

Enniskeane man's bucket souvenir of papal visit

TO MOST PEOPLE it's just a humble plastic bucket, but to pensioner John Joe McCarthy it's a valued souvenir of one of the most fascinating days in his life – the day Pope John Paul II came to Limerick. At a time when the Catholic Church is in crisis and fundamental pillars of Church policy, such as the ordination of women and compulsory celibacy, are being questioned by the majority of practising Catholics, this West Cork pensioner remains deeply faithful to the Church.

So much so that John Joe is planning to present a simple black plastic bucket, which he has had mounted on a slab of marble, to his former school, in memory of the Pope's visit to Ireland more than 30 years ago. On 29 September 1979, John Joe rose at 4.30 a.m., with his late wife Joan and young son, to catch the train to Limerick for the long-awaited visit by the head of the Catholic Church – and brought the bucket with him to Limerick Racecourse.

'I used the bucket to carry my provisions for the day – my lunch, my camera and my binoculars,' he says, quipping that the solid two-gallon bucket, which measures more than 12 inches in height, also served two other important functions. 'I used the bucket to sit on and I also turned it over and stood on it in order to take pictures of the Pope as he passed in front of me in his Popemobile! So the bucket had three functions! I kept it all these years as a souvenir of the Pope's visit to Ireland.' He moved house during that time, from Tipperary, to Mallow and then to the West Cork village of Enniskeane, and each time he moved, the bucket came with him.

However, the announcement in early 2012 that the Eucharistic Congress was to take place in Dublin prompted him to take action. 'I thought about the bucket and I felt I should hand it over to the school where I was a pupil,' he says. John Joe now plans to make a presentation of the bucket, along with a laminated notice that explains the story behind the bucket, to Ahiohill National School, of which he is a former pupil. (He left the school in the 1940s.)

'I originally wanted to have an inscription put on the bucket, but because it is made of plastic this could not be done. Instead I have written out the background to the story and laminated it. I also have a marble slab on which to display the bucket.'

Another reason why he intends to present the bucket to the school, he says, is because the pupils and teachers there have created a museum in a room in the school which celebrates the heritage and culture of the surrounding area. 'It's an excellent museum, they even have a spinning wheel.'

'I will present it to the school in mid-May and it will go into the museum there and will be a memory of the Pope's visit to Ireland.'

CONCERT PROMOTERS CHANGE MUMFORD & SONS PLAN SO RESIDENT CAN WALK HER DOG

THE FULL CLOSURE of Salthill Park for this week's Mumford & Sons concert has been put back a few days. And not for any technical reasons we hasten to add. The organisers of the concert have tweaked their event management plan to take account of concerns of a local resident. The resident from Oaklands, which is nearby but not overlooking the park, was concerned that she would not be able to walk her dog in the park because of the restrictions that were planned from Monday of next week.

The concerns were expressed as part of an observation submission to Galway City Council. In response, concert giants MCD has curtailed the restrictions planned for the park. It had planned to close the entire park from Monday to facilitate the installation of a temporary three-metre metallic wall around the park and to build the stage. But following the doggie concerns, only part of the park will be closed on Monday, Tuesday and Wednesday. The entire park will be closed from Thursday onwards with a partial reopening again on the Sunday, the day after the concert. It is hoped to have it fully reopened on Monday, so Salthill dog walkers can rejoice!

PARKING METER RAIDERS DIDN'T PAY FOR PARKING

GARDAÍ IN ATHY are seeking to put the clamps on a brazen bunch of meter-beaters who relieved three parking meters in the town of a total of €1,300. While the rest of us moan about having to put money in these machines, the culprits in this case were apparently well equipped to get it out, using a drill to turn the meters into handy cash dispensers.

The thefts occurred overnight on a Wednesday night/ Thursday morning, with €400, €600 and €300 taken from the three meters, two of which were located at Emily Square and the third at Meeting Lane. While the total sum involved is substantial, the money would presumably all have been in coins, leaving the culprits literally weighed down by cash. So it's to be assumed that those involved must have had a getaway car in the area. Needless to say, they didn't pay for the parking.

This is the first time a crime of this nature has been committed locally and, in the bid to ensure that it will not be repeated, Athy Gardaí will be continuing their investigations and won't be parking the case any time soon.

Hitting the roof – futuristic, retractable roof proposed for Main Street, Portlaoise

THEY SAY THAT if we could only put a roof on it, we'd have a grand little country, so why not start in Portlaoise? A futuristic, retractable roof across Main Street was proposed by Councillor Jerry Lodge last week, provoking a colourful reaction from his council colleagues. Councillor Lodge made the suggestion during his motion calling for a modern urban renewal scheme in Portlaoise.

Councillors had listened attentively to the well-intentioned motion, but the wheels came off slightly when Councillor Lodge broached the idea of staging festivals. Councillor Lodge said one thing the county did very well was festivals. However, he bemoaned our climate: 'The weather kills us.' As a result, Councillor Lodge proposed a retractable roof be erected on a portion of Main Street. He said it was important to try 'something different'.

Cathaoirleach of Portlaoise Town Council, Willie Aird, quipped: 'We are being different with a retractable roof!' Councillor Aird paused, possibly imagining the retractable roof, before saying to his colleague 'fair play to ye!' Such was

Councillor Aird's delight in the proposal, he later explained it to Councillor Mathew Keegan as he took his seat, having been absent from the council chamber. 'We have gone modern now,' said Councillor Keegan.

Councillor Keegan had a similar motion to Councillor Lodge, which encouraged the council to restore the old Portlaoise town centre as a place of business. Councillor Aird said that he would have to try hard to match Councillor Lodge's idea. After Councillor Keegan had outlined his views on the motion, Councillor Aird offered him an opportunity to articulate his own outside-the-box thinking.

'How can I match that,' replied Councillor Keegan.

'Try it,' urged An Cathaoirleach.

'I would not even try it,' chuckled Councillor Keegan.

Councillor Caroline Dwane offered the memorable line: 'They say, if we could put a roof on it, we'd have a great little country, are we going to start in Portlaoise?'

Councillor Lodge stuck to his guns and added, 'Why not?'

THE GREYHOUND THAT KEPT RUNNING ENDS RACE IN A CEMENT FACTORY

A KILMALLOCK DOG trainer has spoken of his relief after his prize-winning greyhound turned up – at the Mungret Cement Factory. Our sister newspaper the *Limerick Chronicle* reported on how Scala Fiona, owned by Kilmallock man Joe Brazill, had broken free from her collar and ran into the city's night after winning the sixth race at the Greenpark Greyhound Stadium.

Aged just 13 months old, Joe was fearful she might not be able to find food or water at such a young age. But in the early hours of Wednesday morning, Joe's prayers were answered after an intensive search, with the help of Ballyneety trainer Denis O'Malley who searched near the Mungret Cement plant. 'The bitch turned up,' a joyous Joe told the *Limerick Leader* when we rang for an update. 'I was out until all hours looking for her, and I did not get home until after 2 a.m.,' he added. 'I was over the moon when I saw her.'

Scala Fiona made her debut at the Greyhound Stadium on Friday night and won her race in just over 29 seconds. Joe said she is one of the few greyhounds who has recorded a win on her first race. Unfortunately, as Joe was being presented with his trophy, the dog disappeared.

Joe, who owns 20 dogs, always prefixes his greyhound's names with Scala. He brought Scala Fiona in Kilkenny. Asked the value of the pup, he said, 'It is very hard to put a price on a dog, because it is too early. I could not really say. She is just 13 months old, so she has a bright future ahead of her. It is very unusual for a greyhound to be this young. She is one of the few greyhounds to win in her first year.'

Race manager Liam Kennedy said instances of greyhounds escaping from race meetings would be very rare. 'Everything was a new experience for her, and I'd say she just got a bit scared, and headed for the city centre,' he said. He added the prize-winning pup 'would probably be a good breeding prospect after her racing career was finished'.

OUR PARENTS LOVED CORK SO MUCH, THEY CALLED US HOLLY AND TANORA

HEALY-RAE'S ROAD HEARTBREAK – POTHOLES FILLED WITH HIS TEARS

A KERRY COUNTY COUNCILLOR has spoken of his broken heart when he sees the damage being caused to the county's roads.

Councillor Danny Healy-Rae was speaking at the November meeting of Kerry County Council where he said all of the good work undertaken by the council to upgrade the county's road network over the past decade was being undone. He said problems with the roads needed to be tackled before further damage was done by bad weather. 'I have to say that it is breaking my heart to see the damage being done to the roads after all the good work carried out by Kerry County Council over the last 10 to 12 years,' Councillor Healy-Rae said. 'Before that they were in an awful state. Why are we going to allow all of this to be washed away?'

Councillor Healy-Rae said blocked drains were causing roads to be washed away and new potholes were leaving repaired roads in a 'patchwork' state. He called for prompt action to deal with the problem. 'This should be tackled before damage is done. The roads are not being properly drained. On particularly wet days there should be dedicated teams put on roads to assess where there is trouble. Water is flowing on the roads and not going into drains,' he said. 'We will finish up with nothing come spring. Something must be done to save what we have put in place.'

Councillor Healy-Rae also called for the council to form a policy to deal with overgrowing trees and hedges, as damage was being caused to car door mirrors. 'As council management and councillors we are judged by the way our roads are. I am asking for something to be done to protect what we have. We would be a long time waiting to put it back in place again,' he said.

MUM DOUBLES EUROMILLIONS WIN BY PLAYING SAME NUMBERS TWICE!

THE CHANCES OF one small area having two winning tickets in the same Euromillions draw on Tuesday night were explained when a south Wicklow mother came forward to say she accidentally played her numbers twice for the same draw, resulting in her doubling her winnings.

The following day the National Lottery announced that there were two local winners of €59,326 each in Tuesday night's Euromillions draw. It was revealed that two tickets, purchased just a few miles from each other, scooped the match 5+1 lucky star prize of €59,326. In both cases, the player opted for their own numbers and played a €6 ticket valid for two draws.

The tickets were sold at Victor Youngs, Main Street, Carnew, on Wednesday, 4 September, and the other from Dunnes Stores, The Avenue, Gorey, on Friday, 6 September.

Then on Friday it emerged that both tickets were bought by the same player. The lucky winner called up to the National Lottery headquarters in Dublin on Friday to collect her cheque for €118,652. 'I forgot I had already purchased my EuroMillions ticket,' explained the delighted County Wicklow mother, who had accidentally purchased another ticket with the same numbers for the same draw and doubled her winnings.

The lucky mother, who wishes to remain private, opted for her own numbers and played a €6 ticket valid for two draws on both occasions. 'I was doing a quick shop and decided that I should check my ticket,' she said. 'As I checked my ticket, "call the National Lottery" popped up on the screen.'

'I then noticed I had another ticket with the same numbers on it so I checked that also and the same thing happened,' she added. 'Not knowing what that meant, I began to shake and haven't stopped shaking since!'

'I don't think I have stopped laughing since I found out,' she added. 'I am just so happy and elated, it couldn't have happened at a better time!'

After she found out that she had won, she said, 'I called my partner and told him. He said he didn't believe me. It was only when I showed him online that he knew it was true!' Talking about how she might spend her winnings, she said with a smile, 'I haven't been on holiday in 11 years, so I will definitely go away next year!'

Man rams garda squad car with horse and cart

An outing to Cahirmee Fair did not end up a good day for a man when he deliberately drove his horse and cart at speed at a patrol car in Buttevant. The man was sent to prison for two months by Judge Olann Kelleher at a sitting of Mallow District Court.

Inspector Tony Sugrue told Mallow District Court that Gardaí were on duty in Buttevant on 12 July for the annual Cahirmee Fair, and when a patrol car turned onto the Doneraile Road, they were faced with the defendant on a horse and cart. In front of a large crowd, he drove the horse and car at speed towards the patrol car. The man pleaded guilty to engaging in threatening and abusive behaviour.

Solicitor Barry Murphy said his client apologised for his behaviour. He had 'a lot of drink taken' but was pleading guilty to the charge at the first available opportunity. Judge Olann Kelleher sentenced the man to two months in prison for engaging in threatening behaviour.

WOMAN 'RANG 999 TO COMPLAIN ABOUT CHIPS'

A WOMAN DESCRIBED as 'bold as brass' by Judge Kevin Kilrane rang 999 to complain about the quality of her chips, Sligo District Court heard.

Garda Alan Murray told the court that at about 1.40 a.m. he was stopped by the defendant outside Bests Chipper in Castle Street. She put her head in the window and said she had some issues with her food. The garda station had received a number of 999 calls complaining about food.

Judge Kilrane said her behaviour was a disgrace and if she had any decency, she could have come into the court with shame. Instead, she came in and said it 'never happened'. 'Did you ever hear such a ridiculous story,' said Judge Kilrane, adding that she was very lucky she was not going to prison. Instead he fined her €500.

SEVERE

LOCK DOWN

CHIP ALERT

>>LOCATION
>>IRELAND

!!!

4
3
2
1

:CODE RED:

ONE DIRECTION – NOW AVAILABLE FOR WEDDINGS

A GAGGLE OF screaming teenage girls gathered outside the Heritage Centre recently where X Factor idols One Direction were among the guests at a music industry wedding, *The Argus* has learned. Former X Factor winner Shayne Ward was a groomsman at the wedding of tour manager Paul Higgins, who wed Clodagh McGeary.

The happy couple were serenaded by One Direction after they took their vows at the picturesque old church, which is now Carlingford Heritage Centre. Olivia Ryan writes that they also sang the Black Eyed Peas floor-filler 'I Gotta Feeling' at the wedding reception, where they were greeted by gangs of screaming fans.

Arsonist sets himself on fire

AN ARSONIST ACCIDENTALLY set himself on fire as he attempted to burn several cars at a local garage when he dramatically got caught in a sudden backdraft. The fire occurred at Brian Reynolds Car Sales at Green Acres, Carlow. The arsonist was dousing an accelerant on several cars parked at the car sales, then maliciously setting them alight. CCTV footage shows the man was then suddenly struck by a backdraft of flames, receiving significant burns to his face, hands and hair.

Several cars were damaged in the arson attack, causing thousands of euros of damage. Sergeant John Foley confirmed that the culprit has not been identified and managed to leave the scene, despite his injuries. He added that the Gardaí are not aware of any motive for the attack. 'We are appealing for information from the public. The man certainly received burns to the face and hands and his hair was burnt, too. The flashback was big enough to cause considerable burns,' Sergeant Foley added.

No hope of Pope visit to his Irish parish

HOPES OF A PAPAL VISIT by Pope Benedict XVI to north Clare have been dashed by his sudden resignation. The paper reports that: 'Hopes were high in 2010 and in 2012 that the Pope would pop over to County Clare, but these never materialised. It was hoped that he may visit Ireland at some stage in 2013, but after his unexpected resignation, this will not happen.'

But his successor may well visit. Why? Well, the serving Pope is nominally the Bishop of the old Diocese of Kilfenora following a papal dictate issued from the Vatican in 1883. This means that as well as being the leader of the Catholic Church and the Bishop of Rome, the Pope is also the Bishop of Kilfenora and the Parish Priest of Liscannor.

ELVIS RETURNS TO THE BUILDING – IN WATERFORD

When the 42-year-old Elvis died, 34 years ago next August [2011], hundreds of tribute artistes emerged, but Rocky Mills was the original and, as far as several generations of music lovers were concerned, he was 'The One'. Last weekend Rocky celebrated his 70th birthday by doing what he's been doing since the 1960s – performing as Elvis. But there was an unusual guest at the birthday party – the King himself made a ghostly appearance during a power cut!

Towards the end of the night at the Majestic Hotel a very strange thing happened. Rocky was halfway through 'Suspicious Minds' and the audience was in full voice with him when there was a power cut. Rocky and the Band were silenced and the crowd also stopped singing. Then, in that moment of silence before everybody started chatting again, a voice was heard singing the song. The sound appeared to be coming from the ceiling, but there was nothing to be seen. Suddenly, as if the unseen singer realised that he was performing solo, the singing stopped and a deep voice was heard to say in a Southern drawl,'Uh oh, sorry about that, thank you very much.'

People didn't know what to think, but then the power came back on, and when Rocky and the band re-launched themselves into the number, the incident was forgotten. But as the reporter was leaving the hotel, a well-known and respected Munster person came up to him and whispered, 'Now do you believe in ghosts?' The reporter said he did not. The well-known person then replied, 'Believe what you want but I can tell you that was the spirit of Elvis singing along with Rocky. It has happened many times before.' Talk about being all shook up!

RADIOACTIVE CROSS ON ROOF OF CHURCH

HOLY FAMILY CHURCH AUTHORITIES in Ballsgrove have to remove a radioactive lightning conductor from the top of the building. It will cost in the region of €10,000 to undertake the work and the announcement was made last weekend. Parishioners were informed that the Radiological Protection Institute of Ireland has been in contact with the Church and 'that the lightning conductor on top of the church contains radioactive material and needs to be removed'. They added that the material 'must be disposed of through the appropriate channels'.

The conductor has been on the cross on the roof for some years and it provides safe passage for a lightning current to the ground. David Dawson from the Institute told the *Drogheda Independent* on Tuesday that 22 of these rods were imported into Ireland in the '50s and '60s from the UK and only 15 remain, including the one on top of the local church. 'The big danger is that if this came down in a storm or repairs were needed on the roof and it was handled by people, it would give a nasty radiation dose. The dangers would not be clear and others could get harmed removing it,' he confirmed. He said that a new European directive is coming into force in July and the Church needed to act to avoid huge expense.

Artist locked up for paying fine

AN ARTIST WHO overpaid a traffic fine three years ago was arrested as he tried to mount his exhibition. Ramie Leahy, who has an exhibition taking place at Rose Inn Street for the duration of the Kilkenny Arts Festival, said he was 'shocked' when three Gardaí arrived and he was taken by taxi to the Midlands Prison in Portlaoise.

In 2010 Mr Leahy had written a cheque for €290 but the courts didn't cash it because it was €20 over the €270 fine. A court subsequently ordered a bench warrant for his arrest over the non-payment of the fine. 'When they arrested me, they handed me back the cheque that I wrote three years ago.

'In hindsight it is funny but it wasn't funny at the time. I was shocked when they came in and arrested me in front of my daughter. It is unbelievable that garda resources are used in this way.' Mr Leahy returned home a few hours later after he paid the fine and signed a document in Portlaoise.

RAMIE HAS THE LAST LAUGH IN PARKING ROW

Celebrated artist Ramie Leahy who was jailed for a number of hours in August for not paying a parking fine has had the last laugh. The Office of Public Works (OPW) bought one of his paintings for €3,000 after his incarceration, and it is now hanging in the foyer of the very garda station where Mr Leahy was brought on 13 August on foot of a bench warrant after his arrest.

The OPW has confirmed that the painting was purchased for €3,000 under the 'Percentage For Art Scheme', as part of the upgrade of the station where a percentage of the building costs is spent on a piece of art. The painting in this instance depicts the old entrance to the city through Maudlin Street and has been classed as a masterpiece by leading experts in the art world.

COW GIVES BIRTH TO TWO CALVES OF DIFFERENT BREEDS!

FARMER JIM KIRWAN had to check he wasn't dreaming when one of his cows delivered two calves of different breeds in the early hours of Wednesday morning. Jim's wife Grainne saw one of his 70-strong herd of Friesian cows give birth to a Friesian heifer just past midnight on Tuesday night, and minutes later Jim helped deliver its twin – a Hereford bull.

'I never even heard tell of the like of it,' Jim said. 'Only I saw what happened I would have taken a lot of convincing.'

Twin calves are themselves a rare occurrence, but what occurred this week on Jim's farm at Taylor's Cross near Clanagher is more unusual again. The step-siblings both share a mother but were fathered at almost the same time by two different bulls, which Jim runs with his dairy herd, leading to two eggs being fertilised and carried to term.

Grainne explained that she saw the first Friesian calf being born from their house, thanks to a camera installed in the shed the couple use to house cows that are near their due date. 'I kind of thought she was still uneasy,' Grainne explained. 'When I went out and looked I rang Jim from the yard. When he delivered the second calf it was a Hereford. He had to stand up and look at the two of them again. Only that we saw both of them we'd have been looking for another cow.'

Usually, twin calves of differing genders lead to infertility. Jim said he's still in the dark as to whether the same rules apply given that these twins don't even share the same breed. 'It's a new one on me, and I'm milking cows for the last 37 years,' he said.

With now a particularly busy time on the farm the twins haven't been given names. However, Grainne says they've been referring to them as 'The Phenomenons'. Both are doing well, but Grainne said she's a bit concerned about what the Department will think when she tries to register them!

CAVAN FORD CAPRI CLOCKS UP 750,000 MILES!

HOW MANY MILES would you hope to get out of your petrol car before you finally retire it? 150,000 miles? 200,000 if you really looked after it? Cavan car enthusiast Willie McCormick's pristine 1986 Ford Capri has over 753,000 miles to its name – the equivalent of circumnavigating the globe 30 times! 'When you tell them the mileage,' says Willie of people who admire his car, 'they look at you as if to say – are you codding me?'

It's natural to think there may be a touch of a fisherman's tale about such a gargantuan figure, but far from exaggerating, 753,000 is actually a conservative estimate. 'The clock even stopped on it for a wee while – there could be another 10,000 on it, but there's over 750,000 miles on it,' assures Willie of his two-litre model, which was a demonstration car with 2,000 miles when he bought it a quarter of a century ago. Since the clock physically can't register this amount of miles, Willie reverts to a meticulous log book he keeps, to tally the number of miles driven.

'I have every gallon of petrol that ever went through it in the book, and every tyre, every battery and everything else that ever went into it. I keep a note of it. But the clock only goes up to 100,000 unfortunately,' says Willie, who's the president of the Cavan Motor Club. The fact that the clock is only capable of showing 99,999 miles suggests that even the engineers who designed the Ford Capri never dreamed that it could come close to the miles Willie's has driven. So surely it's a case of grandpa's axe – it has had 10 new handles and 10 new heads, but everyone says it's been in the family for years.

Has Willie replaced every part of the engine over the years so effectively it's a totally different car? 'No I have not,' insists Willie. 'There was only a cylinder head gasket skimmed, and I did that last year. That was the first thing I had done to it.' So what's the secret to Capri longevity?

'Normal routine maintenance,' explains Willie. 'That car was serviced every 3,000 to 4,000 miles without fail. She wouldn't go over 4,000 miles without a service – change oil and filter.' When servicing his car, he insists on using only top quality oil and genuine Ford parts for his Capri. This formula has kept him right, not only with his seemingly immortal Capri but also with other cars too. 'I had another, a 1.6 which had 430,000 miles on it. I did a lot of miles over the years when I was on the road all of the time. I never had a problem with any Capri in my life. Never,' says Willie who's currently driving a Mercedes with a respectable 190,000 miles.

As fashions changed, Capris ceased rolling off the production line in 1987, replaced by newer, sleeker models. For Willie, and the many other Capri fans, the muscular car has never lost its charm. 'In her time I reckon I would give it 8/10,' says the Swellan man who bought his first Capri in 1971. 'They are a great car, and anyone I knew who ever had one, I never heard them complain about them in my life.

'I'm into rallying and they are a sporty car. A very comfortable car and a real road-holder. The one I have is a five speed gearbox, which is pretty fast. They were way ahead of their time.'

Does Willie think his car has the Cavan record for the most miles clocked up? 'Well I don't know anyone else in Cavan who would have that kind of mileage,' says Willie, thinking out loud. 'Maybe there are people out there who do a lot of mileage but I've never come across anyone. I saw someone in the paper with over a million miles on a Beetle, but I don't think it was in this country.'

Willie's not hopeful of hitting the million miles mark, as he doesn't drive as much. Indeed this year the Capri hasn't been driven at all, as he's fearful of the corrosive damage caused by the use of salt on the road at the start of the year. 'I didn't want to get the salt on the bottom of it because whatever salt they are using this year is awful. It's digging into cars already. In a few years' time the cars will all be rotten,' he warns.

However, Cavan residents are likely to see Willie's Capri back on the road this week as he taxed it again and intends driving it as his main car Mondays to Fridays. Now that he's back behind the wheel of his pride and joy, does he think a time will come when he has to retire it? 'No I do not, she's going like a bird as the fella says.'

Bandon's boy Norton back for Rebel Week

CORK'S CHATTY CELEBRITY Graham Norton braved the elements last Friday in his hometown Bandon to officially open the Graham Norton Riverwalk. Bandon Town Mayor said: 'It is an honour to welcome home one of Bandon's most famous sons, Graham Norton. We look forward to welcoming Graham home for the occasion and are urging people to come along and join in the festivities.'

Graham, 50, gave a small speech at the Riverwalk at The Bridge, Glasslyn Road before planting a tree at the Community Garden. 'I don't understand what this honour means but I hope that the young people who see my name on this walkway reflect that leaving isn't the same as disappearing and it's not the same as forgetting.

'I would ask you to think of me as you get drunk and fall in the river, indulge in some heavy petting behind the bush or simply bend to pick up your dog's poo – I'm touched to be honoured in this way.'

A KILKENNY 'CAT' OF THE UNEXPECTED KIND

The tale of a large and mysterious cat-like creature prowling around south Kilkenny has reared its head again. In south Kilkenny, the sightings have been recorded in recent years near Mullinavat and Glenmore. One local man described seeing an animal the size of a Rottweiler but 'with the head of a cat' and 'huge eyes and jaws'. One such experience is recalled by Ned Egan, who was driving in his van around 7 p.m. on a summer evening. He watched for about 20 seconds as a panther-like animal ran through a field.

Far from being terrified, he says the experience was beautiful, even ballet-like. And to those who don't believe him, he says, 'I saw it, and I'm glad I did, because I've never seen such a marvellously graceful animal in my life. It was the Rudolf Nureyev of wild creatures, the [Galina] Ulanova of beautiful animals – and stuff the naysayers and disbelievers. Although, in truth, I can't blame them.

'I'd love to have had a witness with me – but people would then only say "two liars instead of one" in that case,' Ned says. 'A camera would have been no use, because of the rapidity. I was a bit in shock when it cleared a fence at great speed, bounced once on the road and cleared the low bank on my right as if it wasn't there. I'd love to see it again – but not at close quarters!'

FARMER TRIED TO PULL WOOL OVER EYES OF GARDA WITH UNLICENSED DOG ... OR WAS IT A SHEEP?

A GARDA WHO investigated reports of unlicensed dogs roaming in the Knock area almost had the wool pulled over his eyes by a farmer who was charged at Castlebar District Court on two charges of having unlicensed dogs. When Garda Peter Sarsfield called to the farm of Patrick Connolly, Rockfield, Knock, he saw two dogs for which licences were produced.

A third dog then appeared on the scene for which there was no licence. When a fourth dog ran from a building, the defendant said to the Garda, 'That's a sheep. Not a dog.' No evidence was produced that it was other than a dog. (Perhaps a sheep dog at that.) Garda Sarsfield said he had no doubt the fourth animal was indeed a dog and not a sheep. The defendant, who was said to be elderly, did not appear in court. A fine of €300 was imposed by Judge Mary Devins.

KNOCK GARDA DEPT
PAWS, DOG
2'7 2014

KNOCK GARDA DEPT
REX, DOG
2'8 2014

KNOCK GARDA DEPT
ROVER, DOG
2'6 2014

KNOCK GARDA DEPT
FIDO, SHEEP
2'7 2014

MAN DRINKS PINT IN COURT – JUDGE CALLS HIM TO THE BAR

IT WAS A PINT that didn't go down too well at all, at all. It might have seemed like a good idea at first for a man to have brought in a pint of the black stuff to court following his dinner during Portlaoise District Court recess, but Lord knows what he was thinking. The fact of the matter was he hadn't a leg to stand on.

The man was to have his case heard during the morning session of Thursday's sitting of the court, but things just didn't work out that way. Instead, his case was put back to the 2 p.m. session. When it did resume and proceedings were underway, the door of the court opened at exactly 2.08 p.m. A stunned silence fell over the court as everyone turned to watch the man swagger into the room with a pint of Guinness in one hand and a rolled fag in the other.

While making his way to his seat, he momentarily paused, looked up at Judge Haughton, bowed slightly and said, 'With all due respects', before taking his seat with a broad smile across his face. The man's defence might not have been the best because, just as he was about to take another sup from his pint, three members of An Garda Síochána took matters into their own hands and escorted the gentleman from the courtroom. When the man's case was called later, his solicitor, Josephine Fitzpatrick, told Judge Haughton, 'I don't think the case will be heard today.'

Twitter and hot chocolate help save newborn foal at County Limerick farm

Twitter is taking over the world and one tweet helped save the life of a newborn foal in County Limerick. Ger Whelan's draught mare foaled on his farm in Bruff on Friday morning, 21 April. Everything went fine until Ger noticed the colt wasn't suckling from his mother. The farmer found that only one of her two teats was working. However, there was very little milk being produced from the one teat and the foal's life was in danger.

In years gone by farmers would ring their neighbours to see if they had any beestings or colostrum for calves or foals. Instead, to get a worldwide audience, Ger thought of Twitter. Not being a tweeter himself, he got in touch with the Irish Horse Welfare Trust and they sent out a tweet: 'FOSTER MARE REQ URG 4 large Draught colt foal. Mare alive but no milk. LIMERICK distance no object: Ger Whelan 086 ...'

It was retweeted over 50 times including by animal lovers in England. While no foster mare was forthcoming, Ger said he got lots of phone calls with advice. And one of those calls with some unusual advice helped to save the day. 'There are different things you can do to help bring the milk down in the mare for the foal. One of them is to put cocoa powder, the same as drinking chocolate, in to the mare's feed. A grain of that in to the mare's feed and that helps her to bring on milk,' said Ger, who is in his early forties. 'Once the milk increased in the one teat, the foal started suckling and now is thriving', says Ger.

'The cocoa powder helped bring the milk down. Whatever it does to the hormones in the mare, it changes the hormones and produces more milk. The two of them are flying it now,' said Ger. 'It was through the help of Twitter that I got tips and advice from different people.

A lot of people rang me and helped me out. I got a big response and it certainly helped,' he added. After this success, Ger is considering joining Twitter but says naming the colt after the social media site might be a step too far!

Once seen on every farm in Ireland, now a draught horse would make you look twice, as tractors made them redundant. But it was the latest advances in modern technology and communication that helped save one's life.

KERRYMAN
TRIED TO STEAL
VIBRATORS
FROM SEX SHOP

A MAN WHO GOT into a fight with a staff member of a Kerry sex shop after he stole two vibrators has been fined over €1,000 at Tralee District Court. Inspector Donal Ashe told the Court that Gardaí were alerted to a disturbance at the Temptations Adult Store at Tralee's Market Street at 4 p.m. They arrived to find two men acting very aggressively and struggling with a third party on the ground outside the shop.

Two of the men had arrived at the shop a short time earlier. One waited at the door of the shop and distracted the shop assistant while the other pocketed two battery-operated vibrators. As he was leaving, he was confronted by the shopkeeper. He denied everything but admitted to taking one, which he tried to pawn back to the shopkeeper. As he was doing this, there was a struggle and the other one hit the floor. Chaos ensued and all three men struggled together over the fallen vibrator.

Defence solicitor Pat Daly said his client and his pal had been drinking and decided to go into the shop 'for the laugh'. 'It was more of a prank than anything else and he can't remember much about the incident. He takes no pleasure in being in court today.' He was fined €1,100 despite both vibrators being given back to the shop in good working order.

LIMERICK MAN WAS 219 YEARS OF AGE

JAPAN'S JIROEMON KIMURA may have become the world's oldest man last week aged 115 years, but buried beneath County Limerick soil is a 219-year-old John Murphy. The tombstone of the mystery man – who is surely a candidate for the Guinness World Records – has been discovered in the cemetery at St John's Church in Knockainey by a local historian. Michael Quinlan was researching his new book on the church when he came upon the unusual inscription.

The oldest grave in the cemetery dates back as far as 1736, but undoubtedly the most unusual headstone is that of John Murphy, of whom very little is known. His gravestone simply reads 'died aged 219 years'. 'When anybody sees it – they are quite amazed,' said Michael. 'The fact is it is written in stone! It is dating from 1784,' he explained of the gravestone. According to Michael, it is 'impossible' to do any research on the individual 'as there is no documentation or parish record going back as far as that'.

Due to the age of the grave, and in turn the faint inscription, the surprising information has escaped the attention of many visitors to the graveyard – until now! 'The news is spreading,' said Michael. 'We have a 20-stop tour of the graveyard prepared and ready, and all these things could come into a little story,' he pointed out.

FARMER REFUSES TO PLOUGH FIELD AFTER HE SEES GHOST

FARMERS BEWARE WHEN you are on the fields this summer. You could spot a ghost wandering a field, as one man did in a field between Rochfortbridge and Milltownpass. According to the *Westmeath Topic*, a farmer is refusing to plough a field after he saw a ghost wandering in it. The paper urges farmers to beware and be aware when they are on the fields this summer.

The eerie late-night encounter with the spirit occurred in an area known as 'Castle Field', on the side of the road between the two villages, while the man was ploughing the field last week. The farmer, who did not wish to be named for fear of being ridiculed (or maybe in fear of the ghost), said, 'I was ploughing the field and it was just an ordinary evening, when I spotted something out of the corner of my eye. I thought it was someone coming up to stop me but then I noticed that it didn't look right. It just seemed to be kind of bobbing up and down.'

The man, from Ballinbrackey, said it looked like a soldier 'with lots of chains around its neck, really heavy chains like you would see on a Norman. Then it took out a cross from around its neck and blessed itself six times'. Unsurprisingly, the farmer refused to continue ploughing the field and left the scene immediately and has not returned since.

But it is not the first time that strange goings-on have been heard of in that area. The area is long rumoured to be the scene of some other-world creatures and there have been anecdotal tales of other unusual events. One story from many decades ago recalls a man trying to bury an animal in the field, but he was unable to break the turf of the field with his spade breaking, despite many goes at trying to do so, while many locals claim that the field is haunted.

Castle Field, which as the name suggests was once the scene of a castle, is also believed to have been the scene of numerous hangings from centuries ago, at around the time of English rule, when protesters and lawbreakers alike were sent to their death and most probably buried at the site.

MAN WHO CASHED FALSE CHEQUES GOES BOUNCING BACK TO JAIL

Mayo ice cream named after Julia Roberts

HOLLYWOOD GOLDEN GIRL Julia Roberts was in Mayo for a few days, and was spotted by stunned onlookers last Tuesday as she enjoyed the attractions and amenities of Westport House and Pirate Adventure Park with her three small children.

The Academy Award-winning actress has been holidaying in the west Mayo area for several days. She has kept a low profile during that time and on Sunday the family visited Old Head beach near Louisburgh, where it is believed they are staying. They stopped at the Ice Cream Parlour and Café at Old Head and queued up for ice cream like everybody else. Despite being instantly recognisable, Julia and her friends and their children were left to their own devices to enjoy their trip to the beach.

'A staff member, Angela Hastings, noticed her first,' explained Julie Parker, who operates the ice cream parlour. 'She was here as a mother, not a movie star; she was very unassuming and was just helping her children have a good time. Noel McGreal came up with the idea to name our most popular sundae after her, so it's now called the "Pretty Woman",' she revealed.

DOG STAYS LOYALLY BESIDE COMPANION'S SIDE FOR THREE DAYS

A COLLIE DOG stayed loyally beside its companion's side for three days when the other dog, also a collie, died at the side of a busy road in Shannonbridge, County Offaly. The ASPCA (Athlone and West Midlands Society for the Prevention of Cruelty to Animals) made the discovery after they received a report of a stray dog. When Inspector Paul McCormack visited the area, he found the collie lying in a ditch beside his dead pal.

He petted the dog, which was terrified, and managed to coax him away from his dead pal, and as he was putting him in the ASPCA van someone stopped and informed him that the dog had been there since the previous Sunday, three days earlier. He hadn't eaten but was beside a stream and so he could have a drink. The collies were later found to be from the same litter.

DANIEL O'DONNELL'S MOTHER KNITS SOCKS FOR THE POPE

THE *DONEGAL DEMOCRAT* had a world exclusive in October 2011 about the latest fashionista to make clothes for the Pope. Nope, it's not Prada, Gucci, John Rocha, Versace, Chanel or St Bernard; it was Daniel O'Donnell's mother Julia! The paper reveals that earlier this year, during the highly successful Donegal Shores Festival in Kincasslagh, Ireland's best-known mother let slip that she had just knitted a few pairs of socks for Pope Benedict XVI.

Ninety-two year old Julia O'Donnell, mother of Daniel and Margo, decided to knit the socks for the pontiff when she had read about the harsh winters expected all over Europe this year. Of course, she used only the very best Donegal wool for the job! 'I just decided to knit a few pairs of socks for the Pope. It would be nice to think that he had a few pairs all the way from Donegal and to be honest I expected to hear no more about it.'

But earlier this week, Julia got a very pleasant surprise when the postman delivered a package to her, which came all the way from the Vatican and included a pair of rosary beads, a personal letter of thanks, a blessing and a signed memento by the pontiff. 'To be perfectly honest I just couldn't believe it at first. I never thought that anybody would take the time to do such a thing. I am absolutely

honoured and you can rest assured that these gifts will have pride of place in my home,' said the formidable Julia.

Her family are all delighted that her knitting skills have been recognised at such a high level. Her son Daniel said, 'I am delighted for my mother. These gifts have been a real tonic for her and have given her a great lift. As long as I can remember, the balls of wool and knitting needles have never been too far away. She really finds knitting so relaxing. It is great to think that Pope Benedict might be wearing a pair of the best of Donegal woollen socks.'

Julia has always knitted, and it's clear that it's a practice she won't be giving up any time soon. 'I have been knitting all my life – socks, scarves and jumpers – whatever. When you had a family of five growing up in west Donegal in the '50s and '60s, it was just the natural thing to do. All my neighbours at the time would have been doing it. We had no shortage of the raw material and our attitude was to waste nothing. Donegal is world famous for its handknits and you will find them everywhere.

'Apart from providing clothes, I actually enjoy knitting. It is one of the most relaxing things you can do and I am told it is becoming popular once again.'

Charleville Castle fire on sale

ANYONE WHO HAS been to Charleville Castle has probably admired the 200-year-old fireplace in the castle's grand ballroom. In a novel attempt at raising funds for the castle and the Shakefest 2014 festival, the fireplace – including fire – is now being made available ... virtually! 'You can enjoy this ballroom fireplace's original beauty and real flames without the smell of smoke, and you can play the Charleville Castle virtual fireplace on any computer or laptop, without having to clean up any ashes afterwards,' fundraisers say.

'Not only is this virtual flames video great for parties or festivities during the Christmas or winter season, the best part of a virtual fire is that the flame never dies down, and you get to experience the authentic beauty and artistry of a 200-year-old castle.'

The virtual fire obviously won't do anything for someone looking for a bit of warmth, but those behind the project promise it has been beautifully recorded with ambient sound and professional video quality. The virtual fire can be yours for €7.50, with the more expensive DVD option setting buyers back €10.50. For that you'll get a one-hour video featuring three separate scenes with natural crackling sounds.

ENTIRE SUMMER HAS NOW BEEN TOO WET FOR DUCKS!

BAD WEATHER FOR ducks has once again forced the cancellation of this year's duck races in Foulksmills and now they won't take place this summer at all. However, organisers are hoping for an Indian summer instead, to allow them to hold the races in September.

Hundreds were expected to gather on the banks of the River Corach on Wednesday evening, but unseasonal and heavy rainfall dampened all plans. The organisers decided on Tuesday morning to call off the Duck Races due to rainfall, but according to Anne-Marie Twomey from the Foulksmills Tidy Towns group, which organise the event, it is hoped to stage the event next month. 'At the moment we have cancelled the duck races but we will see what the weather in September might be like,' said Anne-Marie.

The duck races are one of the longest standing traditions in Foulksmills and unfortunately had to be postponed already this year on 18 July, as the park was waterlogged. The event has been running since the early 1980s and is a firm favourite not only with locals in Foulksmills but also with the wider community of County Wexford.

Council paints yellow lines around parked car

A MOTORIST SAW YELLOW – double yellow – when she returned to her parked car on Thursday to find that the council had actually painted double-yellow lines on either side of her car! And to add to her woes, the young woman had been issued with a parking ticket. The Carlow Vocational School student, who does not wish to be named, was left stunned by the discovery at Green Road, Carlow. The student had been regularly parking in the same spot for the past three weeks.

'She was 100% adamant that the lines weren't there that morning,' her mother told the paper. 'The lines were freshly painted all the way up to her car's tyres and to the car behind hers too. Both of the cars had parking tickets on them. They can't do that!' she added. 'There were no signs up to say that painting was going to take place and no traffic cones – nothing – yet she got a ticket,' the angry mother explained. 'They should have put signs up and certainly not have given out tickets.'

Carlow Town engineer Brian O'Donovan confirmed to the *Nationalist* that there had been works in the area without notice. 'We have to work weather dependently, that's why there was no notice given. We choose a different area when the weather is good, like it was, and get what we need to get done,' explained Mr O'Donovan. 'We did the work there because residents had requested that it be done.' However, Mr O'Donovan accepted that this motorist may have a case for appeal. 'If that was the case, it's completely unfair. The person can write in to us and appeal the parking ticket.'

TENTH ANNIVERSARY BLISS AS LOST RING FOUND DOWN THE BACK OF A COUCH

A WEDDING RING lost to a Corofin couple a decade ago was found and returned to them just in time for their tenth anniversary celebrations. Charlie and Mary Rogers had given up hope of ever finding the ring, which they lost two months after getting married in Renmore in 2001. They had thought they lost it in the US.

However, fast-forward a few years later and Knocknacarra housewife Eithne Murtagh was breaking up a second-hand couch she had bought when she found the ring. It was engraved with the initials M and C, and the date of a wedding. Her husband said it was coming up to the tenth anniversary so she should try and track down the couple.

Eithne contacted the births, deaths and marriages section of Galway County Council, and what the paper describes as 'a very helpful girl called Fiona' found that an M and a C did get married in Renmore Church. The priest who was attached to the parish in 2001, Father Eamon Dermody, was then contacted, and he remembered the couple and wedding clearly, but said they had moved to New York.

Undaunted by all of this, Eithne decided to Google the couple and to her surprise found that their firm, Stateside Solutions, had a Galway office. And who worked there? Lo and behold the happy couple were reunited with their ring.

GARDA TRAFFIC UNIT HAS NO CARS

BAD NEWS FOR the boys in blue in Kilkenny. Gardaí attached to the Thomastown Traffic Unit have no official patrol car assigned to them, making it almost impossible for them to carry out their duties. It raises questions about how drivers will behave in the area the officers are supposed to monitor, from Bennettsbridge to Glenmore. Bizarrely, the nine members of the unit have been given the temporary use of a car which would not be capable of pursuing another vehicle in a high-speed chase.

The officers, who are thought to be extremely unhappy about the situation, are more or less confined to the barracks because of the scenario, which highlights the Government cuts in garda budgets. A senior garda source told the *Kilkenny People* that the unit was not able to properly police the area. 'People can drive around at whatever speed they want and it is highly unlikely they will be caught,' he said, adding that it was also unlikely that there would

be cars available to man checkpoints over the coming weeks. 'There is a bank holiday weekend coming up and normally there would be a high garda presence on the roads but I don't see how that can happen this year,' he said.

The nine-member unit have been given the 'temporary use' of one vehicle – a Galaxy marked garda car – but that particular car would not be able to pursue another vehicle. 'It would be unsafe to drive at high speeds in a chase. In any case that vehicle is attached to the forensic section of the station so we do not have first call on it. If it is at another incident then our unit has no vehicle to use. We are not able to get our own so the roads are left unpoliced. We are begging for cars, the men are available but there are no cars for them to use,' he said. Previously they had two vehicles, but they were not replaced after they exceeded 300,000 kilometres a month ago.

LOO COSTS
ALMOST AS MUCH
TO RUN AS TOWN

IT'S COSTING ALMOST the same amount of money to run the public toilet in Bagenalstown as it is to run Bagenalstown itself. At a Thursday meeting, the Town Council's budget of €50,888.80 was agreed by the members while on Friday the cost of running the town's superloo was agreed in Carlow County Council's budget. On Thursday night Councillor Joe Manning said, 'It's costing €50,000 a year to run the town council and €40,000 a year to run that toilet. It's crazy.'

However, Councillor Denis Foley said it would cost €180,000 to break the 15-year lease for the superloo. He added that the old toilet in the town had been vandalised repeatedly whereas the superloo wasn't being vandalised. He said it was so clean 'you could bring anyone into it'.

Councillor Liam O'Brien also disputed that it cost such a significant amount to run the superloo. 'From my recollection it costs between €15,000 and €18,000 per year. I don't think it costs anywhere near €40,000.' However, Town Manager Seamus O'Connor agreed the cost of running the town's superloo was 'close enough' to Councillor Manning's figure.

Councillor Paddy Kiely said he was in Cahir recently and 'wanted to spend a penny' and he came across 'a grand public toilet. There was nothing lavish about it and there was room for two or three lads to go into. It was a massive little toilet.' The debate goes on.

SENATOR TAKES LIPSTICK GRAFFITI ON THE CHIN

A DISPARAGING COMMENT scribbled in lipstick on the front window of Labour Senator John Whelan's offices in Bull Lane, Portlaoise, over the weekend, was shrugged off by the Senator as an 'act of love'. The words 'Ass Hole' were written in red lipstick on the window. His personal secretary and county councillor Lisa Delaney, who works from the office, said she had not observed it on first opening the office on Monday morning.

When asked to comment on the slogan, Senator Whelan said later that day, 'What did it say? "Ass Hole". What was it written in? Lipstick. It was done in love. What colour was it? Red. Labour red. It was an act of love.'

IS COUNTY COUNCIL TRYING TO DISPOSE OF WEXFORD?

WEXFORD COUNTY COUNCIL has unwittingly put the county up for sale. One of its latest tenders, published on Friday, is entitled: 'Invitation for tender for Financial, Legal and Advisory Services for the disposal of Wexford County.' However, having been alerted to the notice by the *Wexford People* newspaper, the Council decided the Model County is not going to be disposed of, and they swiftly changed the notice to what it was supposed to be – an invitation to take over its refuse service.

THE HOLY WELL THAT'LL NEVER RUN DRY

A LOCAL MAN has invented a holy water font that will never run dry! It was while visiting houses in the locality and finding the traditional holy water fonts dry in many cases that Connie Gallagher came up with an initiative that has already resulted in interest and sales in this county and beyond. After undertaking some research on the subject, the Derrybeg man started work on a dispenser fitted with a unique metal tip that's attached to a container which doesn't require refilling for months.

'I would be going into a lot of houses and when you're leaving you get into the habit of blessing yourself but half of the holy water fonts would be empty. And people would be saying "I filled that yesterday or the day before and it's already gone dry". That's when I began thinking there must be some way of overcoming this problem.'

And at the end of June, the Sleeghan-based father-of-two commenced development of the holy water dispenser that won't run dry any time soon. Not a dry font in the house, it might be said. 'It's simple but not that simple to get it right. The brains of it are in the dispenser cap,' Connie points out.

The dispenser – its patent pending at present – comes complete with a support structure that can be hung on any wall and includes a special design. 'There's a choice of fifteen different designs including saints such as Saint Bernadette and Saint Anthony, the Sacred Heart and Our Lady.' There's also a choice of three different colours: mahogany, pine and white/cream. Only the very tip of the actual dispenser is visible when it is attached to a wall surface. 'It lasts for months before it has to be refilled,' he insists.

Connie has carefully handcrafted each one of the dispensers he has already produced – and demand has already exceeded expectation. He has brought his initiative to the far reaches of the county and it's also on sale in Derry. 'Eventually I hope to hit the whole country with it.' The Derrybeg man was previously involved in the manufacturing of patio slabs, but the economic downturn largely put paid to that in recent years. But his unique dispenser is set to pave the way for a future of holy water fonts that will never run dry.

Trespassers claimed to be jogging to lose weight

TWO CASTLEBAR BROTHERS claimed to be out jogging in the dark in an attempt to lose weight when confronted by Gardaí near a machinery yard in Turlough. The brothers appeared before Castlebar District Court charged with trespassing.

Inspector Joe McKenna told the court that Garda Martin Friel responded to a report of a vehicle acting suspiciously near McGrath's industrial waste yard at Gortnafolla, Turlough, Castlebar on 22 February last, at 8.50 p.m. The report also said voices could be heard from within the yard.

The court heard that Garda Friel saw a vehicle reversed up a small laneway near the yard and shortly after spotted the brothers walking towards him. When Garda Friel asked them what they were doing, they claimed they were out jogging trying to lose weight.

Judge Devins heard that two diesel tanks in the yard had been tampered with and footprints were found close to the tanks. The footprints were preserved and a plaster cast was made of them. They matched the prints of the running shoes worn by both of the accused. 'CSI Mayo,' Judge Devins observed.

ESB POLE IS NO DRIP WHEN IT COMES TO POWER SHOWERS

IT NEVER RAINS but it pours – particularly if you happen to be standing beside a certain ESB pole in Dromina that produces a cascade of water which gives new meaning to the term 'power shower'. That was the claim by Councillor Bart Donegan (FF) at the Kanturk area meeting on Friday morning. He said the wooden pole located on Main Street is something of a 'peculiar thing'.

'I got calls about it and didn't believe it myself until I went out and had a look of it. I'm telling you the water flowing off it when it's raining, you could have a shower under it,' he said. He said he was particularly concerned as it was a pole that had lighting. He was advised that the best port of call was to make contact with the ESB Networks Department.

After the meeting, speaking to the *Corkman*, Councillor Donegan said, 'When it's dry, it's just a pole. There's nothing running off it, it's normal. But when it rains, well that is different. I couldn't believe it myself.'

MAN CLAIMS CAKE PUT HIM OVER THE LIMIT

A TRALEE MAN who pleaded guilty to a charge of drink-driving at Killarney District Court told his solicitor he had only one drink on the night he was stopped by Gardaí and it was 'brandy in a cake that put him over'. The man was fined €125 and disqualified for a year by Judge James O'Connor.

PLEASE, GOD, MAKE IT STOP RAINING: BISHOP CALLS ON PEOPLE OF DIOCESE TO PRAY FOR SUN

WHEN ALL ELSE fails get down on your knees and pray. That's the message from Bishop of Ferns Denis Brennan who, after weeks of depressing summer rain, has asked everyone to pray for sunshine at masses this weekend. The appeal is a response to numerous calls from parishioners who have inundated the Diocese with requests for weather-related prayers, according to diocesan secretary Father John Carroll. 'Requests for prayers for fine weather are many at present,' said the Bishop. 'They include the very heartfelt of the farming community who play a vital role in our society and our economy.'

The Bishop said many local farming families are experiencing strain and anxiety as they grapple with the prospect of further bad weather and a threat to the annual harvest. He asked parishioners to pray for fine weather this weekend and to offer solidarity to those who depend on agriculture as they experience 'acute distress and fear at present'.

The Bishop invited people to say the following prayer: 'All-powerful and ever-living God, we find security in your care and love for us. Give us the fine weather we pray for and need. May the harvest be secured and the hard work and efforts of so many people come to fruition. We ask this through our Lord Jesus Christ.'

DUBLIN AND CORK GET JOBS, WHILE NAVAN GETS SILAGE

Clare litter louts to be attacked with drones?

DRONES, SUCH AS those used by the US and Israeli military, could be used as Clare's newest weapon in the war against litter, one local councillor has suggested. The remote-controlled surveillance devices, which have gained notoriety from their use in international war zones, have been put forward as a possible solution to fly-tipping in the county, with a claim that drones are already being used on the continent for this purpose.

Councillor Johnny Flynn came up with the proposal. After hitting out at the 'disgusting' behaviour of people who litter the county's roads, he said government grants could be used by the local authority to send a drone into the air to identify the culprits of illegal dumping. Last year, grant funding was used by Clare County Council for the deployment of a mobile CCTV unit. It's now time to step it up, says Johnny.

'I would suggest that the council consider applying again this year and (instead of CCTV) consider using drones, robotic flying cameras, that could be used to look out for fly-tipping. We have to come down very hard on these people. There are a million bags of rubbish unaccounted for in this county,' he said. 'This could be a very effective weapon to deal with these anti-social scoundrels.' He added that a tough stance needs to be taken on anybody found illegally dumping.

'Anybody involved in fly-tipping and serious and persistent anti-social behaviour should have the benefits of living in an open and modern society restricted. For example, any person whose vehicle is found to be involved in fly-tipping should lose their driving licence for 20 years.'

KERRYMAN CRASHED CAR WHILE ADMIRING FEMALE GARDA DUO

A VALENTIA ISLAND resident who leaned out of his driver's window to make 'jovial' remarks to female Gardaí on duty in Tralee managed to grab their attention in no uncertain way when he crashed his car into the vehicle in front of him, Tralee District Court heard.

Gardaí told the Court that the man crashed because he was too intent on impressing the Gardaí rather than on the road in front of him. 'Two female Gardaí were on duty in Princes Street when they heard a fellow shouting from the opposite side of the road. He was the driver of a car and was hanging out his window yelling at the Gardaí. It was jovial enough,' Inspector Martin McCarthy told the court. 'Two seconds later he ran into the car in front of him.' His solicitor said he was very complimentary to them; he just took his eye off the road. The man was fined €350 having pleaded guilty to careless driving.

LIBRARY GETS OVERDUE BOOK BACK – 58 YEARS LATE

A BORROWED BOOK has been secretly returned to Carlow County Library an incredible 58 years after it was first loaned out! Flabbergasted staff in the library on Tullow Street, Carlow, were left open-mouthed when the book was dropped onto their front desk by an unknown lady.

The book, *Fra Angelico: The Master Painter* by Aengus Buckley, was lent out on 20 April 1955. It was returned to a shocked staff member, Lionel De Froy, who is on work experience from Belgium, on 28 May. The book in question features black and white illustrations of the early Renaissance Italian painter's work. Fra Angelico lived to be 60, which is two years longer than the time the book was lent out for.

It is understood that the book, which has only ever been loaned out once, was discovered in an attic, but details are sketchy. Good folks that they are, Carlow Library staff did not charge any late return fees – but if they did, the borrower would have had to cough up €301.60, which is ten cents a week since April 1955. 'We are just very pleased to get our book back,' said a spokesperson from the library.

Hotel sails away

WARRENPOINT IS GETTING a new 100-bedroom hotel – but, bizarrely, the facility will just be passing through the south Down town. In five weeks' time the hotel, which is being developed by contractors McAleer and Rushe, and Milltown-based firm Sipfit, will be loaded onto a container vessel at Warrenpoint Harbour and shipped to the Shetland Islands. This is possible because the structure is being developed in individual, modular rooms that can be easily transported and pieced together.

Speaking to the *Newry Reporter*, Eamonn Higgins of McAleer and Rushe said the primary reason for the nature of the project was the lack of sunlight in the islands, which lie some 60 miles north of Scotland. 'The main reason was the weather in Shetland – such as the lack of daylight,' he said. 'But also that we could do it here. Shipping it out, when completed, only represents 2 per cent of the cost of the whole job and if we had built it there we would have had to ship out all of the materials.

'The completed rooms are currently being stored in the harbour estate. 50 of the 100 rooms are there – fully fitted out. The rest will be finished in a few weeks. Then on 28 February they will be loaded onto a container ship and sent to Shetland.' But whilst south Down may not be gaining some much needed hotel beds, the local economy has still benefited substantially.

COUNCILLORS TO 'STEAK OUT' KEBAB SHOP

THE ISSUE OF A takeaway restaurant on Linenhall Street, Castlebar, operating without planning permission took a comedic twist at the June meeting of Castlebar Town Council. Independent Councillor Michael Kilcoyne raised the issue of the business still operating as a takeaway outside the hours permitted in its planning permission. Town engineer Sean Higgins informed the meeting that he had himself attended the area outside of his normal working hours to see was it breaking its planning permission and was waiting on CCTV footage from the Gardaí so he could move ahead with proceedings.

Independent Councillor Frank Durcan told the meeting that 'I'll go there between 3 a.m. and 4 a.m. myself and have a look and give evidence in court if I have to with Councillor Kilcoyne.' Councillor Kilcoyne told Councillor Durcan that he had no problem at all doing that.

EXPECTING A DELIVERY ON CLARE ISLAND?

A BOX WITH no name on it has turned up in the shop. It was left in Roonagh with a delivery for the shop, presumably by courier. It has been there for about ten days. For more information, contact Pádraig at the shop.

THE WHISTLING DONKEY OF DINGLE LEAVES COURT IN TEARS OF LAUGHTER

A BUSKER, BALD TYRES and a whistling donkey left the presiding judge, Gardaí, solicitors and even defendants in tears of laughter in Dingle District Court on Friday as they heard of the unlikely series of events that led to three road traffic charges being brought against a man. Well-known Dingle street entertainer Déaglán Ó Muiris became the unintentional source of comic relief at the sitting, when Garda Frank Scanlon outlined the scene that greeted him when he stopped the busker for driving with four bald tyres.

Garda Scanlon told the court that having noticed the worn tyres on Mr Ó Muiris's Hiace van, his attention was immediately drawn to the inside of the vehicle, where he saw a donkey looking back at him. He proceeded to tell Judge James O'Connor how the said donkey is part of Mr Ó Muiris's renowned busking act and is regularly seen with the defendant in Dingle.

When asked by the chuckling judge what the donkey did as part of the act, Garda Scanlon told him he played the tin whistle, causing an outburst of laughter in the courtroom. Solicitor Pat Mann told the highly entertained judge that his client and his donkey are a regular double act at Dingle pier and that Mr Ó Muiris is 'a very good natured man'. He said that after being stopped by Garda Scanlon, he paid €350 for four new tyres for the van.

Withdrawing one of the charges, Garda Scanlon said he was very familiar with Mr Ó Muiris and had come across him on numerous occasions, adding that he had one previous driving conviction dating back a few years. Mr Mann quickly interjected, telling the court that that offence was for driving his Hiace van and not his donkey. Garda Scanlon agreed that the tyres had been replaced and concluded his evidence by telling the judge that the donkey has been retired for the winter. The defendant was given until May of next year to pay €300 to the court poor box to avoid a conviction for the bald tyre offences.

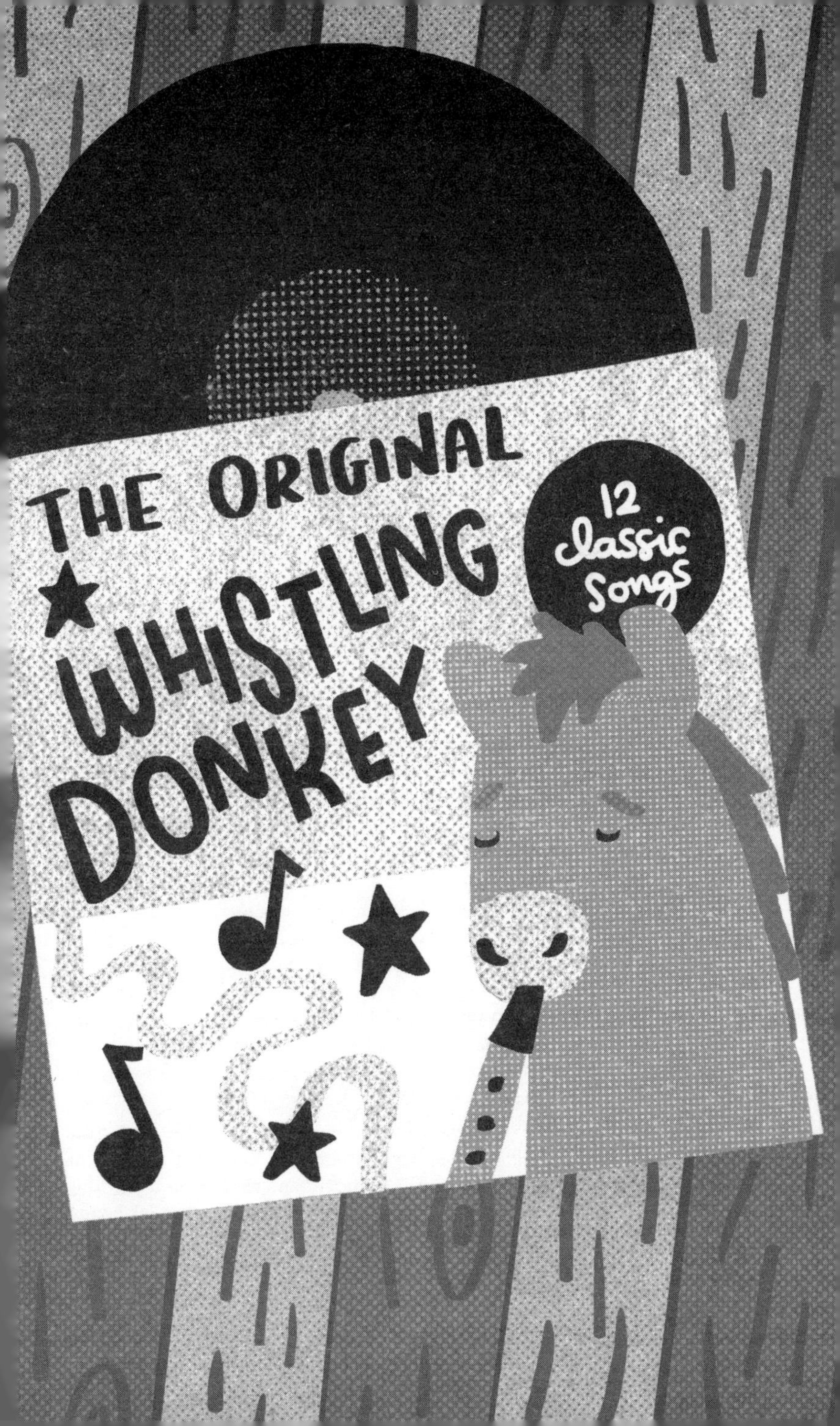
THE ORIGINAL
WHISTLING
DONKEY
12
classic
Songs

'CASHEL MAN' IS OLDEST BOG BODY IN EUROPE

LAOIS HOLDS THE unusual record of having the oldest bog body discovered in Europe. The remains are of a young man killed in human sacrifice around the year 2000 B.C. This date means that what is now called 'Cashel man' is the oldest body with flesh on it that has ever been discovered in Europe. Tests carried out on the remains of the bog body discovered in 2011 in Cashel Bog have proved it to be the oldest in Europe.

The findings have been reported by Eamonn Kelly of the National Museum in the latest volume of *Ossory, Laois and Leinster*, the history journal covering mainly counties Kilkenny and Laois.

So surprised were the experts at the date of the body that a second series of tests were carried out in England on the peat found above and below it and these tests confirmed the body's age. It had been thought initially that the body might have been that of an English Elizabethan soldier involved in the Nine Years War of the late sixteenth and early seventeenth century.

When the initial carbon dating results were returned, however, it became clear that something of extreme historical significance had been discovered. Dr Kelly maintains that the wounds on the body, and the fact that it seems to have been tied down beneath hazel rods, all point to the man being the victim of a ritual sacrifice. 'All the indications are that the human remains from Cashel Bog tell of the fate of a young king who, through folly or misadventure, was deemed to have failed to appease the goddess on whose benevolence his people depended, and who paid the ultimate price,' said Dr Kelly.

OUR MESSAGE IN A BOTTLE FOLLOWED US ALL THE WAY HOME

A COUPLE OF Ballyvourney pupils were surprised to open a letter sent to their school last week to find a message they threw into the sea off the coast of England two months ago. Doireann Ní Lionáird and Darren Ó Ríordáin were in a group of 12 students in fifth year from Coláiste Ghobnatan, Ballyvourney, who took part in a school exchange with Collège Édouard in Rostrenen.

On 23 March last, the group left for France, travelling to Brittany from Cork via ferry. 'When we were given some free time, everyone except for Darren and I decided to go to the cinema,' Doireann told the *Corkman*. 'Instead, Darren and I decided to get something to eat. When we were eating, we noticed that the ketchup came in a small jar. That gave us the idea to write a note, put it in the jar, and throw it overboard.'

Back in a cabin, they wrote the note on a napkin and stuffed it in the jar. 'By then our friends had returned, laughing at our plan but still joined us in throwing it overboard,' said Doireann. 'Having passed England, we went up on deck at the rear of the ship and threw it into the water, never for a minute thinking that we would see it again,' she explained.

On the morning of Wednesday, 22 May, a letter arrived at their school, addressed to the pair. 'I opened the letter and let out a shriek of surprise as I found our napkin-note that we had thrown into the sea two months earlier,' said Doireann. 'There was a post-it note attached, explaining that it had been found at Lahinch Beach, County Clare. A phone number was also given.

'Everyone was amazed when we told them of our note's incredible journey and urged us to get in contact with the person who found it,' Doireann said.

The next morning, two months to the day since the bottle was thrown from the ferry off the coast of England, the pair called the man who found their note.

'We were delighted when a man named Mr Oliver Liddy answered, telling us how he had found the note when he was on holidays in Lahinch Beach two weeks ago,' she said.

GUN IS THE ONLY ANSWER TO CROWS

A KNOCKNAGOSHEL FARMER, who claimed he is being tormented by crows damaging his bales of silage, has succeeded in his appeal against a garda decision refusing to grant him a gun licence. Michael Lenihan, of Meenganaire, Knocknagoshel, told Castleisland District Court that he needed a shotgun to scare away crows that are costing him up to €400 a year in damage to bales of silage. He said all other measures to keep the crows away had failed.

'I used to paint the bales with white paint and that worked for a while, but not any more,' he said. 'They only way to scare them off now is to fire four or five shots in the air.'

Inspector Fearghal Patwell said that one condition of being granted a gun licence is that two people must act as referees, and in the case of Mr Lenihan these two people had withdrawn at the last minute. Neither he, nor the defendant, could explain why that had happened. Inspector Patwell also told the court that another issue of concern was why, after farming all his life, Mr Lenihan suddenly needed a gun now.

Mr Lenihan's solicitor Patrick O'Connell said his client had complied with all other conditions, including installing a gun safe and completing a shooting proficiency course. He said if Gardaí had an issue with the referees, they should produce them in court. Judge James O'Connor allowed Mr Lenihan's appeal, saying 'the law will decide the rest'.

LOST ENGAGEMENT RING FOUND IN POTTED PLANT ... AFTER 15 MONTHS

AMAZING COINCIDENCES HAPPEN all the time, but it was in the Arboretum Garden Centre in Leighlinbridge that a most romantic story recently unfolded. 'It's quite Titanic-esque, really,' Fergal Doyle of the Arboretum said. 'Who would have thought that this would happen?'

Some 15 months ago, an elderly lady visited the centre with her son and spent some time browsing through some of the hundreds of plants, flowers and shrubs that were for sale. However, when it was time to leave, she discovered that her precious engagement ring was no longer on her finger. The pair were convinced that the ring had slipped off her hand on the journey from the car into the shop, so they alerted the staff to their crisis.

The sizeable car park was scoured, as were areas inside the huge garden centre. But no matter how much the staff helped, the ring could not be found. When it was time for the lady and her son to go home, she left her contact details with the Arboretum in the hope that the ring would be found. Months and months passed, but there was still no sign of it.

Then just last week, by the strangest twist of fate, it turned up. A customer, whose family has a grave in Borris, has a tradition of calling into the Arboretum en route to the cemetery to pick up a fresh plant to place on the grave. She had visited the grave about 15 months ago, having called into the garden centre and bought a potted plant. Her sister had returned home from America in recent weeks and the pair decided to make the journey down to Borris cemetery. As usual, the woman popped into the Arboretum to pick up a replacement plant to freshen up the grave.

In Borris she busied herself replacing the plants that she'd bought the previous year but, just as she was lifting the old one out of its pot, she felt something hard and circular in the soil. To her amazement, it was an engagement ring. She rightly concluded that the ring must somehow have gotten into the pot in the garden centre, so she immediately contacted the staff to tell them about finding the treasure.

'The woman had obviously bought a plant that the other lady had browsed through,' Fergal explained. 'Who would have thought that the ring would have fallen into a plant? We'd scoured the car park looking for it.' Staff members who'd hunted for the lost ring the previous year recalled the elderly woman and her son and how devastated they were at the loss. However, due to another twist of fate – a cruel one, this time – the log book in which the woman's name and phone number were written had been destroyed.

'Her details were lost because the log book was destroyed by water damage,' Fergal continued. 'The staff remember that she used a wheelchair and that she was with her son. It's quite Titanic-esque, isn't it? How many elderly ladies lose their engagement ring?'

The details of what the ring actually looks like are top secret, but Fergal does say that it's 'quite old-fashioned'. Now there's a quest to reunite the lady with her long-lost ring. 'Our customers visit on a weekly, monthly or even yearly basis and this woman could be from anywhere,' said Fergal. 'We're trying to reunite the ring with its rightful owner and we're appealing for people's help with this.'

The King of Tory Island says Duchess of Cambridge would be very welcome

The King of Tory Island, Patsy Dan Rodgers, says the Duchess of Cambridge would be very welcome on Tory Island.

The beauty formerly known as Kate Middleton met Greencastle native Paul Gill, when she launched the *Royal Princess* cruise liner in June. Paul, who works on the ship, told *Peninsula People* magazine she came to the bridge to meet the ship's officers and, noticing his badge with the Irish Tricolour, asked him where he was from. He recalled, 'When I told her I was from Donegal, she said, "I hear it is lovely, I would love to visit there some day".'

Patsy Dan Rodgers commented, 'She's very welcome on Tory Island. Why not? Ireland and England are closer than they've been in a long time. We had an increased number of English visitors this year and we'd love to see more.'

FAILURE IN ATTEMPT
TO TUNNEL INTO
LIMERICK PRISON

OVER THE YEARS, there may have been some prisoners who dreamed of tunnelling their way out of Limerick prison. But on Tuesday workers were unsuccessful when they tried to tunnel into the prison, after they hit hard rock. Staff from the Office of Public Works (OPW) were carrying out preparatory work for the installation of a new sewerage scheme to replace the old Victorian one in place.

When they tried to tunnel underground the prison, they reached a dead end. A hole had been dug from the inside of the Mulgrave Street jail and the hope was it would meet another one on the other side. But these plans fell between a rock and a hard place when workers found there was no way through. Work had to be abandoned for the day following this.

Publican Jerry O'Dea, whose business is next door to the prison, said his customers found the spectacle hilarious. 'I just happened to be in the pub yesterday morning, and we heard a lot of noise of dumper trucks going around, and huge drilling machines going in and

out. After making general enquiries, we found out they were attempting to drill out from the prison, underneath the prison wall. They dug the hole on the inside, and also dug the hole on the outside, so the two would meet,' he confirmed.

Around six engineers were sent home for the day and will come back in the coming weeks to start the job. Mr O'Dea added, 'I believe they have to come back with more elaborate drilling equipment which apparently costs up to €90,000 a day to provide, so it looks like they have a big project on their hands. I just hope they get off to a better start than they did yesterday'.

A spokesperson for Limerick City and County Council confirmed that the OPW had commissioned a new sewer connection. The work – which will involve the resurfacing of roads – was scheduled for August, because of the fact schools are off, and the roads are more likely to be quieter. When in place, the new sewerage system is likely to serve the new courthouse when it opens in Mulgrave Street next year.

LIMERICK PUB THIEVES ESCAPE THROUGH PRISON

IT IS BELIEVED that a gang of thieves who stole a large amount of cash and a number of liquor bottles from a city centre pub on Saturday morning accessed the property – and made their short-lived escape bid – through a yard attached to Limerick Prison.

Publican Jerry O'Dea admitted it was unusual to hear of thieves 'breaking into a prison', after his business was targeted and three cash registers robbed at around 6 a.m. A spokesman at Roxboro Garda station said that two men were 'caught in the act' and arrested in the immediate aftermath of the incident.

The yard houses the accommodation block for prison officers as well as storage facilities for the Mulgrave Street jail. It is enclosed behind a 10-foot wall on Mulgrave Street and it is believed the raiders may have scaled this obstacle before and after raiding the pub, for which they had to climb a second perimeter wall. The pub is sandwiched between the yard and the secure prison complex, and Mr O'Dea said his business was previously targeted by thieves who gained access from prison property.

'We did have another burglary here about 10 years ago and we believe it happened in that way,' said Mr O'Dea. 'It's disappointing but in a way I suppose it's humorous too and all the talk in the pub and on the street today is that while you'd often hear of fellas trying to break out of a prison, you'd never hear of them trying to break into one.'

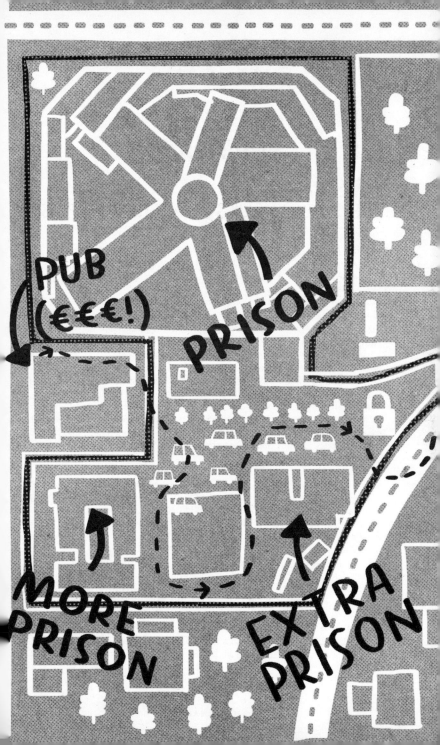

US RAPPER KANYE WEST BREWS UP A STORM IN PORTLAOISE CINEMA

CINEMA-GOERS WERE expecting a few shocks on screen when they went to see the sci-fi flick *Prometheus* in Storm Cinema on Thursday, but the biggest twist of all was when a Grammy award-winning artist sat down next to them. The rapper decided he'd be better chillin' with the homeboys in Portlaoise, when he was in Ireland recently for a couple of sold-out shows at the 02.

Shocked locals spotted Kanye as he took his seat for the sci-fi flick. The man himself was said to be a little uncomfortable that he might be discovered so he pulled up his hood in a vain effort to conceal his identity. He might have been successful if it wasn't for his darn 12-strong entourage sitting around him!

The paper gleefully reports that the US rapper enjoyed his cinema experience in Portlaoise so much that he returned on Sunday afternoon to watch the same movie. Social networking sites like Twitter were flooded with reports of Mr West being in the cinema on Thursday night, and the paper managed to get a picture of Kanye chillin' with some local young lads. A spokesperson for the cinema confirmed Mr West did indeed visit the cinema to watch *Prometheus* 3D.

The rapper was staying in the luxurious Ballyfin Demesne at the foot of the Slieve Bloom Mountains prior to headlining a show with Jay Z in Dublin. The gorgeous Ballyfin Demesne was recently voted the top resort in the world by a US magazine and has attracted the likes of Julia Roberts since it opened.

While the rest of his time in Laois is clouded in mystery, internet speculation is rampant as to what other activities he got up to. Darts in Ryan's Pub, perhaps? A trip to the Rowl 'n' Bowl? A visit to the site of the legendary Blue Bridge? Ireland must be known for the quality of its rural cinemas, as when he was in Ireland, the King of Pop Michael Jackson allegedly visited the cinema in Mullingar.

HOLY GOD, 21 'NUNS' DRINKING AFTER HOURS

ONE OF THE chief organisers of Listowel's record-breaking Nunday has found himself in hot water with the law, after allowing the committee back to his bar for celebratory drinks after finally wrapping up the event at 2 a.m. After a long night ensuring all the details were properly registered for their Guinness World Records attempt, a local publican allowed his fellow organisers back to his pub for a few drinks to celebrate. The event had not only attracted over 1,400 'nuns' to the town on 30 June last – smashing the previous world record – but also raised over €26,000 for Pieta House.

Local Gardaí were alerted to the activity when two men were seen leaving the bar at 4.05 a.m., and inside were met with the surreal sight of 21 'nuns' drinking while the publican had left to drive others home. The unfortunate series of events resulted in the publican being brought before Listowel District Court this week where he pleaded guilty to after-hours. 'I could plead that my client couldn't refuse nuns, but I don't know if that will get me anywhere,' solicitor Maurice O'Sullivan said in his defence.

Despite inquiring if the committee had broken the world record, Judge Angela Ní Chondúin fined the publican €200 but said she appreciated that he had been put under 'terrible pressure' on the night.

The €5 million bridge that won't close

IT WAS CONSTRUCTED at a cost of €5 million, but marine traffic is still unable to pass through the access bridge on to Achill Island. The bridge has been impassable for the past month and is likely to remain that way for some weeks yet, with locals describing the situation as 'disgraceful'. The swing-bridge – named after Land League patriot Michael Davitt – has been plagued by problems since it opened to traffic in December 2008. Ironically, the original bridge was replaced because it failed to close properly.

On one evening over the Christmas, tailbacks at the time reached six miles as locals were prevented from returning home after school and work. The bridge has not been opened to boats since and it will be some time before it's fixed. A spokesman told the *Western People* they will have to select a time when there is little or no traffic – possibly late at night – and conduct tests to ensure everything is in working order. Local Councillor Michael McNamara says, 'When you pay for something you expect it to be working properly. And at a price of €5 million you would expect it to work. There is no excuse.'

BRING M&S TO LIMERICK FOR THEIR FRILLY KNICKERS, URGES COUNCILLOR

LIMERICK COUNCILLOR ORLA McLOUGHLIN urged city officials to do all they can to bring Marks & Spencer into the city before the year was out — because its underwear 'has a certain je ne sais quoi'. She admitted she has a soft spot for the lingerie section in the popular chain.

During a debate on the much-talked about issue at this month's City Council meeting, Councillor McLoughlin disagreed with Councillor John Gilligan's protests that bringing the British retailer into the city would be 'economic suicide'.

In a passionate contribution to the meeting, Councillor McLoughlin said, 'We should do everything we can to bring Marks & Spencer into town. I am a lady. I like clothes in all shops. In particular I like the lingerie section in Marks & Spencer. It has a certain je ne sais quoi.'

In response, Mayor Gerry 'Ginger' McLoughlin, her father and former rugby legend who played for Ireland and Munster, agreed. He said, 'But you will have to explain to me what je ne sais quoi means, Orla.'

KERRY PEOPLE MAY HAVE LANDED IN US LONG BEFORE COLUMBUS

NEW RESEARCH SUGGESTS that a tribe of Kerry people lived side-by-side with Native American neighbouring communities in what is today the Carolinas and Georgia – long before Christopher Columbus sailed the ocean blue. It came to light after comparisons were made between a mysterious rock carving found on a farm in Georgia and carvings found on the Dingle Peninsula. Researchers found the puzzling glyphs and concentric marks on the famous Reinhardt Boulder to match ones on the Dingle Peninsula.

Kerry's potential link with pre-Columbus America came to light in new research on a famous book, *De Orbo Nova*, written in 1521 by Spanish historian and professor Peter Martyr d'Anghiera. The Spaniard interviewed as many Native Americans as he could about the history of the area before the arrival of Europeans. Many of his subjects spoke of a tribe called the Duhare living in the Carolinas and into Georgia. Taller than Native Americans and Spaniards, their hair was red and their most famous leader was a tattoo-covered giant called Datha.

A chronicle of Native American language found translations for all native words, until they got to the region of the legendary Duhare, as many words associated with native life in the area stumped researchers. That was until they began comparisons with the Irish language, finding the exact same word for deer — 'fia' — had been in use in the region among the Duhare. Their research also brought them to a translation for the name of Datha himself, derived from the Irish for 'colour'. This certainly chimed with his painted appearance.

Martyr d'Anghiera also learned that the Duhare (possibly meaning 'from Ireland' if their language was indeed Irish) lived much more peaceably with natives than the later Spanish colonists. While the research is far from definitive, it is another tantalising glimpse into what might have been, along with St Brendan and Viking lore.

Cameras hidden in sods of turf catch litter louts!

KERRY COUNTY COUNCIL has come up with a brilliant way of catching litter bugs and illegal dumpers. They have taken to hiding spy cameras in sods of turf and rusty tin cans! Several dumpers have been caught redhanded at remote north Kerry locations, and the Council are predicting that many more will be caught in the coming weeks, as hidden cameras are deployed at a number of remote spots in the county.

The cameras are inserted into cans and then stuffed into sods of turf. Senior Planning Engineer Tom Sheehy has hailed the new filming method as a triumph, as identifying litter bugs was the biggest obstacle to prosecuting offenders in the past. Of the 583 cases of illegal dumping investigated by the Council staff last year, there were just 12 convictions. He expects several to be before the courts soon.

CRIMINAL FOUND HIDING UNDER ATTIC INSULATION

GARDAÍ ARRESTED A MAN after he was found hiding under the insulation in the attic of a house, Gorey District Court heard. A court report in the *Gorey Guardian* says the court heard how Gardaí raided a house at Rochestown at 7.45 a.m. that morning. They searched the house thoroughly, as well as the attic, but didn't find him. A second search of the attic revealed he was hiding in a remote corner under attic insulation, and two officers had to go up to take him down. 'It would appear he was attempting to evade arrest,' the court was told.

LONELY DINER
UNABLE TO
FOOT THE BILL

A MAN WHO thought his luck couldn't get much worse after being stood up by his dinner date at a Dingle restaurant soon realised his troubles were just beginning when he had to admit he had no money to pay for his meal. The embarrassing end to the man's night out was played out at Dingle District Court on Friday, where it emerged that the ditched diner had been banking on his lady friend to foot the bill at the Chinese restaurant – despite the fact that he had invited her on the date!

The 39-year-old not only had to deal with his date not showing up but also had to face the owner of the Tír na Rí restaurant and tell him he had no money to pay for the two meals and wine he had ordered in anticipation of her arrival. Gardaí were alerted and he had to repeat his embarrassing tale and was subsequently charged with making off without paying for goods valued at €44.

Defending his 'unfortunate client', solicitor Pat Mann outlined the sequence of events. 'The bottom line is that the defendant had invited this lady on a date and she didn't turn up. Because hope was all the time "spring-rolling" in his heart, he decided to order for two and even sent Mr Wong [the restaurant owner] to the cellar for wine,' he told Judge James O'Connor.

After intense questioning by the intrigued Judge about what he ate and whether he enjoyed it, the man said he did until five minutes before it was time to leave. 'By then I was getting concerned about what I was going to say because I knew I had no money. I tried to explain but it was no good. I told them I would pay it back,' he said.

Although the incident happened in February 2012, the man has still not cleared his bill, with his solicitor conceding that 'the food is well cold by now'. He will, however, pay the bill this week he assured Judge James O'Connor, who adjourned the case until September.

MAN FOUND

IN CHRISTMAS

TREE AFTER

NEW YEAR'S

EVE DRINK

OH, HOLY FLIGHT!

THE 75-YEAR-OLD 'FLYING NUN' who completed a 10,000-foot skydive at Galway Airport last week has said she's unlikely to make a 'habit' of jumping out of planes. Presentation nun Sister Patricia Wall, who lives in the County Tipperary village of Ballingarry, undertook the 2000-kilometre-per-hour freefall skydive for Aware on Friday, having planned the jump since September 2012.

Sister Wall, who battled with depression many years ago, says she wanted to let people know that there is help out there for people who suffer from depression. 'There are a huge number of groups ... that are giving support, so you're never too far from support, but of course, when you're in the depths of depression, it's hard to reach out, isn't it?' said Sister Wall.

Sister Wall first approached Galway-based Skydive Ireland last September and was told that her age was no impediment to her completing the dive, provided she obtained a doctor's cert. By that stage, it was late in the skydiving season, so she deferred the jump until this summer.

Recalling the jump itself, Sister Wall said the whole experience was a 'blur'. 'The first 20 minutes, going around Galway Bay until you got high enough was grand, that was lovely. But when he opened the door and then the cold air came in and then the photographer went out, then you're whooshed across the floor and out before you have time to think! It is a blur.'

Sister Wall said she was not afraid at any stage but did admit to feeling relief when she landed safely, aided by professional skydive instructor Dean Cocozza of Skydive Ireland. The septuagenarian skydiver said that she felt she would be able to savour the experience more if she undertook a second jump, but joked that another jump might be harder on her instructor than on her. 'I sent an email to Skydive Ireland and I said that I couldn't put Dean through the trauma again, trying to mind me!'

So far, Sister Wall's heroic efforts have raised almost €26,000 for Aware and for local projects in her area, and she is hopeful that when everything is accounted for, that figure will top €30,000.

While she may not take to the skies again any time soon, she shows no sign of slowing down yet in her charitable work, with a hot rod racing day planned in nearby Dunkerrin. 'Sure if I go up there, I'll have to do a round of the track, won't I? We'll see!'

Long arm of the law delivers Daingean baby

Tullamore-based Garda Nicola Gleeson probably didn't think the long arm of the law meant her duties extended to delivering babies, but that's exactly what she found herself doing last Monday night in Daingean.

Mother-of-three Niamh Longworth saw the 15 August due date for her third baby come and go. One week later – on Monday night – baby Longworth made her intentions felt, however, and like her previous two births Niamh expected she was in for a long labour. With her lorry-driver husband Damien working, she called sister-in-law Imelda over to keep her company at about 10.30 p.m. Just a couple of hours later Niamh knew she wasn't going to be able to wait, and after remembering seeing two Gardaí on Daingean's Main Street earlier, her brother Stephen asked them to come to the house to provide a garda escort on the way to Portlaoise hospital.

Niamh's labour was too far gone to go to hospital, however, and so with the help of her husband who had just arrived in the door, Garda Nicola Gleeson, her sister-in-law, mother, and paramedics over the phone, she gave birth to a healthy baby girl called Mia at 1.40 a.m. on Tuesday morning.

Describing the eventful birth, Niamh's husband Damien said he was expecting things to move so slowly he debated stopping for a snack in Portlaoise on his way home from Kilkenny. 'She was so calm that when I was going through Portlaoise I was thinking to myself would I get something to eat now because I'm going to be in hospital all night,' he laughed.

Arriving home at 1.15 a.m., Damien found himself taking over the position of head midwife at the birth of his child and even though he said he was at the births of both of his older children Aaron (6) and Finn (14 months), it didn't prepare him at all for the job in hand. With help from Garda Gleeson and Imelda, and taking instruction from paramedics Ollie and Gerry, Damien helped baby Mia make her way into the world in the front hall of her own new home.

Though both Imelda and Damien say Niamh was extremely calm, neither Damien nor Niamh have any plans to have more children at home, or even in hospital. 'We said we'd keep going until we had a girl,' Damien explained.

Niamh and baby Mia were bundled up and brought to Portlaoise hospital immediately after the birth, and came home again last Wednesday. Looking back on the whole thing Damien said he's just glad it all worked out. 'A thousand things could have happened, but nothing went wrong, thank God.'

STOLEN EXORCISM CHALICE RECOVERED

The church chalice used in one of the most infamous exorcisms in this country has been recovered following its theft from a church in County Wexford. The chalice of Father Thomas Broaders is said to have been used to exorcise the devil from Loftus Hall on the Hook Peninsula, and it was one of a number of items stolen recently from four churches in Ramsgrange, Foulksmills and St Mullins.

Most of the items stolen from the churches were not recovered, but the discarded exorcism chalice was found by a man out walking his dog in St Kearns, Saltmills. Father Bernard Cushen said it was a great relief to have the 1742 chalice back, and even he wondered if its role in the 1800s-era exorcism proved too much for even the most faithless thieves to take in.

According to legend a stranger who was looking for accommodation at Loftus Hall on a stormy night was invited in to play cards. During the card game a lady bent over to retrieve a fallen card and was shocked to discover a cloven foot. It is said that the stranger vanished through the ceiling in a puff of smoke.

Loftus Hall was then exorcised by Father Thomas Broaders whose powers worked. Sadly, the building in which the legend is associated was levelled to the ground in 1870 and a mansion was erected in its place. The property, which was successfully run as a country hotel by the Devereux family until the late '80s, is currently for sale.

Def Leppard serenade Louis on his 83rd birthday

Louis Mullen was sitting in bed, enjoying a quiet cup of tea and reading the paper, on the morning of his 83rd birthday recently, when the phone rang. It was his son Aidan calling from Melbourne to wish him a happy birthday. After chatting for a while, Aidan said, 'Hold on Dad, someone here wants to wish you "Happy Birthday".' Louis then heard a group of people singing and realised that he was being serenaded by Def Leppard!

Aidan is a guitar technician with the world-famous rock group, who were touring Australia at the time. 'I think this must be a record of some sort,' said a delighted Louis. 'Not every 83-year-old has all the multimillionaire members of Def Leppard singing for them from ten thousand miles away.'

His son has been working for Def Leppard for over two years, having previously worked for Metallica. 'He's a great guitar technician and is very much in demand in the business. He has travelled all over the world and they are just back from Japan and hopefully he will get back home to Nashville in time for his wife's birthday next week.' Louis and his wife Bonnie, who live in Riverstown, have met with the musicians from Def Leppard on a number of occasions. 'They are really great guys,' he says.

BAMBI, THE COUNTY LIMERICK DEER WHO THINKS HE'S A CALF!

AN ORPHANED DEER, which turned up in the backyard of a County Limerick family-run guesthouse, has been adopted by a herd of cattle and now thinks he's a calf. 'Bambi' arrived into the yard of the O'Neill family home at Castleoliver Farm in early January. With no food or sustenance – his mother is suspected to have been shot by hunters – the young deer began suckling from one of the cows.

'He is just one of them now,' explained Alyce O'Neill of Castleoliver Farm and luxury cottages which are located outside Ardpatrick. 'We just went out one morning and he was there in the field with the cattle and of course we have named him, needless to say, Bambi. He was obviously very young because he was actually suckling from the cows,' she added.

The deer has become so attached to the cattle that everywhere they go, he follows. 'When they move between the fields he goes with them,' said Alyce, a mother of four. He even nudges the six cows and six calves out of the way to get at the hay and on occasion ventures up to the back door of the family home to have a look.

Around six weeks ago during a spell of very wet weather, the cattle broke out and ventured up to the house. Hot on their heels was, of course, Bambi. 'They came up the drive and I looked out the kitchen door and there were all the cattle and the deer in the middle of them looking in the door at me. He is a real pet,' said Alyce.

The O'Neills endured an anxious wait earlier this week when Bambi, who takes his name from the famous Disney story, disappeared for a period after scampering into the forest adjoining the O'Neill's land. Thankfully, he returned safe and sound on Wednesday morning and is back in the company of his beloved cattle. 'I was actually upset,' said Alyce of Bambi's disappearance. 'He gets a bit nervous with other people. He doesn't mind me when I go out to see the cattle and he now stays for his food,' she explained. One of Alyce's seven grandchildren, nine-year-old Leon, calls to see Bambi every weekend.

DUBLIN'S LUCKIEST LOTTO PLAYER WINS AGAIN!

IT WAS A CASE of *déjà vu* for a lucky Dubliner who cashed in another big lottery win recently, his second in the space of three years. The charmed local picked his second winning ticket in January, almost three years to the day after he collected the Lotto jackpot of €2,825,374 in 2008.

Lady luck shone for the second time after he won €500,000, through a €10.50 Quick Pick ticket bought in Spar, Carpenterstown, in Dublin 15, on the day of the Monday Million draw on 17 January. He only realised his luck last month when he found his ticket and realised that it hadn't been checked.

'I found a bunch of unchecked Lotto tickets, ones that I had bought over the last month and I decided to bring them to my local shop to check them,' he explained to the Dublin People Newspaper Group over a glass of champagne in the winner's suite of the National Lottery offices. 'When I scanned the Monday Million ticket, I was totally shocked to realise I had won again. I jumped straight into my car and came here to collect my prize.'

Despite his lotto bonanza back in 2008, the Dubliner had continued to play the Lotto but had no winners until last month. 'I plan to continue playing Lotto and Monday Million; who knows? Maybe I will be back here to collect another prize within the next three years again,' he laughed.

Thief pulled a pint as he robbed a nightclub

A MOUNTRATH MAN was caught pouring himself a pint whilst robbing a Portlaoise nightclub. The court heard how the man had broken into Egan's nightclub on 8 April last, around 12.45 a.m. Detective Edel Hanley said, 'He had gained access and poured himself a pint before taking two bottles of Hussar vodka worth €36 and a bottle of Bacardi worth €42.' Judge Gerard Haughton sentenced him to a combined total of 18 months, alongside a driving ban.

LOCAL ACTOR CROWNED CLOONEY LOOKALIKE

A LOCAL ACTOR beat off stiff competition to be crowned 'lookalike' to Hollywood heart-throb George Clooney and will get the once-in-a-lifetime opportunity to attend the Oscars in Los Angeles in March.

David Glendon will fly over to the prestigious event with Kilkenny-based filmmaker and historian Gabriel Murray, who organised the competition. 'My company Olympia Films were allocated four tickets to the Oscars in March so we will be taking David with us. He will also be attending the Irish Film and TV Awards, which are held in Dublin next month. We took into consideration in deciding the winner that David is a local actor,' added Mr Murray, who is on the voting jury for the Irish Film and TV Awards.

The competition was held in Dylan's Whiskey Bar on John Street on a Friday night. In the run up to the event entrants were asked to submit a photograph where they posed and dressed as the legendary actor, whose Kilkenny roots were confirmed late last year. Some 783 entries were received from all over the country and the organisers shortlisted it down to five, before announcing the overall winner that night.

'I decided to do it for a bit of craic, for the fun of it,' said winner David Glendon. The 27-year-old, who is currently single, is no stranger to acting, having recently set up Firebird Theatre. 'I have been involved in nearly [every] amateur group in the city. Our next production is on in Cleere's in March,' he said. 'I am delighted to have won. To go to the Oscars, well that would be anyone's dream come true,' he said.

Mr Murray discovered last year that George's antecedent was a Nicholas Clooney from Windgap. There was some previous investigation in 2008, but the baptismal certificate of Nicholas Clooney, George's sixth-generation ancestor, had not been found. A Fás community employment scheme recently computerised all the birth records in Ireland. When Gabriel discovered the relevant certificate last November, it revealed that Nicholas Clooney was baptised in Windgap church on 23 July 1829 and was from Knockeen, Tullahought.

The comments section of the *Kilkenny People* newspaper related to this article are worth a look. A rep from a George Clooney fansite said, 'We were wondering what criteria were you using to judge the competition because although he's a good looking man, he doesn't look a whole lot like George Clooney', whilst another asked if Stevie Wonder was the judge.

IT'S PAINTBACK TIME!

A YOUNG TULLAMORE artist, who stole shotguns and whiskey from a house in Ballycumber, has been ordered to create a portrait of the courtroom he ended up in, complete with judge, solicitors and Gardaí as punishment. Outspoken Judge Seamus Hughes handed down the novel sentence to the young man on a Wednesday's sitting of Athlone District Court.

During the case, Judge Hughes was shown a portfolio of the defendant's artwork, which he deemed 'quite excellent'. Stating that he was known for occasionally coming up with unusual punishments, the Judge said he wanted the defendant to 'do an artist's sketch of the courtroom, focusing in particular on the practitioners of the court'. He wanted the defendant to 'work hard at this' and expected it to be done in time for the 19 December sitting of the court. 'It can be a Christmas present' for those working at the court, he said.

'I often see in serious murder trials that they don't allow photographers in court but have sketch artists instead. I want this man to do an artist's sketch of the courtroom, focusing in particular on the practitioners of the court.

'I think it would be nice to have a portrait of this kind, because the practice of the court might be quite different in 10 or 20 years' time.'

The defendant said the process would take some time, as it had taken him about 10 hours to complete each of the pieces that were in his art portfolio. 'I can give you 240 hours if you like,' said the Judge, referring to the maximum term of community service which is sometimes given to defendants. He said he would not be surprised if the case made banner headlines in 'the *Sun*, the *Daily Mail*, and those other papers that I don't read', but all he was seeking to do was to get the defendant to use his talents.

Judge Hughes has form. In October 2011, a youth who spat at a garda squad car was ordered to wash the squad car once a week for a six-month period. Also in 2011, two men who came before him were instructed to save turf and deliver it to the Society of St Vincent De Paul as punishment for their misdeeds. In 2010, Judge Hughes attracted national media attention because of a novel punishment he handed out in Donegal. A man who called a Garda a 'Mayo w**ker' was ordered by the Judge to climb Croagh Patrick as a mark of respect for his fellow Irish people, especially those in the line of duty.

'I'M BEING FOLLOWED BY A BOA CONSTRICTOR'

HORSELEAP RESIDENTS SINEAD O'NEILL and her boyfriend Paddy Barrett got the shock of their lives when they discovered they were sharing their home with an unwanted guest – a six-foot boa constrictor. The young couple, who moved into the rented house four months ago, discovered the snake when they were about to start cleaning out their shed. Their reptilian guest was wrapped around an old bed frame that was being stored in the outbuilding.

Student Sinead said that they think the animal belonged to the former tenants who had kept exotic pets. 'It had been living up there for six or seven months. His enclosure was in the shed (when we moved in) but we were told that the snake was gone. Obviously it wasn't.'

The boa had made quite a cosy little nest for itself in a cardboard box in the shed, dragging in some hay for added heat and comfort. When hunting prey, boas grab with their teeth before suffocating their quarry and consuming it whole. Sinead believes that it kept itself alive by feeding on the shed's previous occupants. 'We noticed that there was a lot of swallow nests but no swallows.'

When the animal-loving couple, who have two cats and two dogs, started ringing around to try and get someone to take away the boa constrictor, Sinead says they had trouble getting people to believe them. 'When I told the guards they asked was I on drugs,' she laughed. Eventually, Dublin Zoo put her in touch with the Reptile Village Zoo in Kilkenny where the snake is currently residing.

Zoo Director James Hennessy, who travelled up to Horseleap to capture the animal, says the snake is as strong as an adult and could inflict serious, if not fatal, injuries on a small child. As for Sinead and Paddy, they are still wondering how someone would move house and not bring all of their pets with them. They are also hoping that there are no more undetected lodgers about the place. 'I can't understand how you would leave a six-foot boa constrictor behind,' says Sinead.

Rock star urges public to 'wake up'

A CHARITY INITIATIVE by the staff and students of St Louis Grammar has unearthed the exciting hidden history of one of the Kilkeel schoolteachers. Moved by the devastation in the Philippines following Typhoon Haiyan, the school linked up with the SERVE charity to produce the song 'Now I Know', which was written by senior teacher Tim Brown, his wife Catherine and the school's music teacher Mrs Dearbhla McDonagh, and performed by A-level music technology pupils.

Speaking to the *Reporter*, Tim revisited his previous career in a band that had a number one album, which yielded an instantly recognisable single. Born in Wallassey near Liverpool, Tim was the bass player of the Boo Radleys, whose 1995 single 'Wake Up Boo!' still regularly graces the national airwaves. 'It tends to be other teachers who tell the students (about the band),' he said. 'They have all heard the song.

'I started playing guitar when I was 11. We were in a band from 15 and played our first gig at 15 as well. We dreamt we could make a career out of it.

'After the band, I ran a studio in Liverpool, I was also working to sustain it. Then I had to think of what I was doing in future and I saw that they were looking for IT teachers in England. I did a year's teaching in Liverpool. My wife is from Belfast and after her father died she wanted to move home. I ended up getting a job teaching at St Louis and have been here since.'

CRIMINAL GANG ATTACKED BY A FERRET

A CRIMINAL GANG bit off more than they could chew when they attempted to steal animals from a rural Cork farm – and were attacked by a ferret.

Macroom District Court heard that Michael Casey (23) of 9 Brookfield Green, Tallaght, Dublin, was one of a number of men who entered the yard of a house at Ballyhandle, Crossbarry, and attempted to steal a number of items and animals worth €950, including two greyhounds and ferrets.

The whole incident was recorded on the householder's CCTV system, and Judge James McNulty described the footage of the robbery during the prosecution as 'truly remarkable'. He noted that one of the ferrets 'locked jaw' on one of the culprits during the theft.

The gang were spotted near the house following the theft and reported to Gardaí by a passer-by. Mr Casey was found guilty of theft, entering with intent to commit an offence and intoxication in a public place. Judge McNulty said that Mr Casey was part of a gang that 'robbed, pillaged and defiled the country home of country people'.

Spooky goings-on at Limerick's Milk Market

SOMETHING VERY SPOOKY is happening in Limerick's 200-year-old Milk Market. Strange glowing lights have been captured on one of the market's 15 CCTV cameras, which some believe are ghostly spirits, or 'orbs'. The footage emerged when staff handed over tapes from their CCTV cameras to Gardaí after the market was broken into in the early hours of Friday, 27 January.

Strange luminous lights were clearly visible from 4 a.m. on one particular camera – camera six, which is located in the arch above the main gate. For more than an hour and right up until the second that the break-in occurs, the lights are plainly visible on the cameras, jetting in and out of the shot, changing speeds and moving in irregular directions.

Milk Market Manager David O'Brien was perplexed. 'We have looked at the footage, it defies logic, there seems to be no rhyme or reason to it – we have looked at it and it leaves us baffled, very baffled,' he said. 'I am as broad minded as the next person, it is puzzling me, it is puzzling everybody else, I am not somebody who goes down the road of thinking it is hocus pocus stuff, but everybody who has seen the footage is mesmerised by it, it is very different,' he added.

A local fortune teller who does readings in the Milk Market believes the light in the footage is an 'orb'. 'I have seen the footage and it looks like an orb, which are spirits,' said Tina Scully. 'In the manifestation of a spirit, they begin first as an orb. There is a long history attached to the market, it has a Famine history and workhouses and a lot of bad things went on there and souls can get trapped like a time warp between worlds, they can't pass from one to another.

'There are energies in the market place — I am absolutely convinced of that,' she added.

A local security guard, who has stayed overnight in the market when concerts have taken place, concurred that he had seen 'moving lights' in the Milk Market which 'freaked' him out. 'I was getting a feeling that someone was watching me. I just saw a bright light in the corner, constantly moving, on the left-hand side, over towards the gate,' said the guard, who did not wish to be named. 'I know other people down there have said the same. It is like a moving light – I could see the shadow of something down on the market floor walking from gate to gate,' he said.

KERRY PEOPLE CANNOT NAVIGATE ROUNDABOUTS

ROUNDABOUTS PRESENT TOO much of a challenge for many Kerry drivers, according to a county councillor in the *Kerryman* who wants better road markings to help people avoid going around in circles. Fine Gael County Councillor Bobby O'Connell called on the council to 'put proper markings on roundabouts to advise drivers which lane they should be in'.

Apparently many motorists are getting confused when trying to navigate their way around roundabouts, particularly in regard to getting in lane. 'They're confusing for drivers of all ages. It's very easy to say "get in lane", but it's the straight one that is causing a lot of confusion,' Councillor O'Connell said. He suggested that the root of the problem was that roundabouts didn't even exist when many Kerry motorists got their licences decades ago. Suggesting that the drivers' problems might be shared by council management, he added, 'People say we should know the rules of the road, but I'm sure that if I went to the top table here it would be very embarrassing!'

Amelia home safe after solo flight

A LOCAL SWORDS resident is feeling relieved after his pet parakeet, Amelia, was found in Dublin Airport. The bird was reunited with its owner after airport workers spotted the bright blue and green parakeet on the ramp where aircrafts embark and disembark passengers. The pet had gone missing from its home in Swords four days earlier.

'I was locking up the aviary last week when she flew out over my head. I was so worried for her because I didn't think she could survive the frosty temperatures. She is one of a breeding pair and her partner was clearly missing her,' said Alexander Fitzsimmons, who was over the moon to hear his bird had been found safe and well.

'When she flew out, it was getting dark and it was a frosty night. There really wouldn't have been a chance for her to survive, we thought either the cold or bigger birds would kill her. Since coming back, she is still exhausted but is safely in her cage,' he said.

It was during a routine patrol that Patrice Dorney of the Dublin Airport Airside Operations Unit was surprised to find the bird. The parrot, a plum-headed parakeet, appeared to be uninjured but was hungry and dehydrated. The airside staff quickly set about finding out where the parrot had come from, despite the bird having no markings or tags. After ringing several pet shops in the area, they struck gold when they contacted Kinsealy Pet Store.

'I'd been in the pet shop two days beforehand, so when someone from the airport rang the shop, they knew to contact me. When I got the call I was delighted,' Mr Fitzimmons continued. Since her adventure, the parakeet has been named Amelia after Amelia Earhart, the first woman who flew solo across the Atlantic Ocean – another lady who loved the adventure of flight.

SAMURAI SWORD ATTACK IN LISTOWEL

THREE YOUNG LISTOWEL people had a terrifying ordeal on Sunday night when they were attacked by an older man brandishing two samurai swords in the centre of town. The man was arrested and no harm was caused to any of the young people involved in the incident, although they are understood to have been quite shaken by the ordeal. It is understood that the samurai swords were replicas and not made to cause injury. Gardaí described the swords as 'quite blunt'.

NUMBERS ADD UP AS TRIPLETS REACH 12 ON 12/12/12

It's a rare combination of numbers: 12 years old on 12/12/12! And when you have two other siblings to celebrate the same event with, it's inordinately more amazing. For this is the birthday triplets Jack, Diarmuid and Micheál Cahill celebrate on Wednesday, with dad John and mom Brenda, at their home in Mullingar.

Jack, Diarmuid and Micheál Cahill – whose mom Brenda comes from Moyvane and dad John from Knocknagoshel – are making world history this week as they celebrate a birthday that is in every aspect extraordinary. The number of statistics this event defies is dizzying. Not only will they celebrate their birthday on a threefold date that won't happen again for nearly 100 years, but their age chimes perfectly with it and they just happen to be triplets! Now living in Mullingar, the three brothers are taking it all in their stride while being quietly chuffed as the significance of their big day sets in among their school friends.

'We didn't really realise the significance of it ourselves until Seamus Roche in Moyvane texted me some months back to say Moyvane would have to have a big celebration,' mom Brenda laughed.

Brenda, who comes from Brosnan's Bar in the heart of the village, says the excitement at home is every bit as much as in Mullingar. Four grandparents in Kerry are proudly smiling on – Mary and Tom Cahill in Knocknagoshel and Jerry and Nodie Brosnan in Moyvane. 'The boys are very excited and we're throwing a big birthday party for them and they're also looking forward to coming home for a week on St Stephen's Day. They have a very strong Kerry identity of course, especially when it comes to the football!' says Brenda.

Unlike the mirror-image birthday numbers, Jack, Diarmuid and Micheál are completely different. 'They're not identical, they're not the same height and their personalities couldn't be more different!'

Frightened feline Freeway escapes death by a whisker

THE *NORTHSIDE PEOPLE* and *Southside People* newspapers don't often print the same story, but they were united in print with the tale of the kitten who escaped certain death on the M50 back in August 2011. The kitten had a lucky escape when she was plucked to safety off the busy M50 motorway. The Dublin SPCA carried out a dramatic rescue when the kitten found itself lost and alone in the central reservation of Ireland's busiest motorway.

The cat, named Freeway by the staff in DSPCA, was spotted by passing motorists, and was frozen with fear as cars hurtled past at 100 km per hour. Ambulance driver Lisa Kemp was dispatched to try to save the terrified kitty after a call was received by the animal welfare agency. However, after arriving at the scene, Ms Kemp quickly realised that the speed of the traffic would make it impossible to get to the cat on her own. Calls were made to local and national media urging motorists to slow down while Lisa waited for the Gardaí to arrive.

'Every time a car went by, he flattened his ears,' Ms Kemp recalled of those frightening moments. 'It was obvious he was absolutely terrified. My heart was in my mouth, I couldn't get to him. The traffic was going too fast and I feared he would run and be hit. I could just visualise it. We called the Gardaí and while I waited for them to arrive, I was just willing Freeway to stay put. The Gardaí were brilliant. They stopped the traffic and I ran with the cat basket, grabbed him and ran back.'

Utterly exhausted after his close brush with death, Freeway was later taken by his rescuer to the DSPCA centre in Rathfarnham where he was later reunited with his grateful owner. 'I really want to thank the Gardaí and all the media who got the word out to slow down,' Ms Kemp added. 'Without their help who knows how horrible this could have been.'

Shackleton's Athy biscuit takes the biscuit

FORGET YOUR FIG ROLLS, your Jaffa cakes or your custard creams. When it comes to biscuits, arctic explorer and Kilkea native Ernest Shackleton's biscuits top the lot. It may not have figs, an orange filling or a chocolate topping, but a 104-year-old biscuit fetched a whopping £1,250 at a Christie's auction in London last week.

However, this is not the most valuable biscuit Shackleton had in his rations. A partially eaten morsel, which was the last biscuit he ate on his journey to the South Pole sits on display at the Athy Heritage Centre. In fact, this was the biscuit that was found in his pocket. That tasty ration was bought for 7,637 old Irish pounds in 2001.

Seamus Taafe, Director of the Shackleton School in Athy, which is based at the Heritage Centre, explained, 'Even though the one that was sold at Christie's was more intact, the one we have is of more historical significance. That biscuit was one of many thousand they brought on their trip. The one in Athy is the one that he had left in his pocket. It was towards the end of his journey and they were crossing the mountains of South Georgia. It was the last biscuit he ate and it ended up in his pocket.'

The half-eaten biscuit was kept in a cigarette box and was passed down through the generations of the family before it came up for auction. 'At the time we were very lucky to have a very generous supporter so we were able to buy it,' added Mr Taafe.

ENQUIRY INTO 'HAM SANDWICH' ATTACK AT PARADE

AN OFFICIAL ENQUIRY is to be launched as to who flung a ham sandwich from a float during the St Patrick's Day parade in the city. The sandwich, reportedly made from brown bread and accompanied by some brown sauce, is being forensically examined as to its contents and further examined as to the evidence of its origin. The sandwich came flying from a float as it passed the viewing stand and dignitaries were said to be less than impressed.

BALLINAGLERA MAN TO THE RESCUE FOR YOUNG MAYO FAN ON ALL-IRELAND FINAL SUNDAY

ALTHOUGH THE DAY ended in disappointment for the Mayo supporters who travelled to Croke Park to see their team take on Donegal, for one nine-year-old from Castlebar there was reason to celebrate, as he was given a ticket by Ballinaglera's Ray Gilmartin shortly before throw-in.

TJ wrote to the *Leitrim Observer* to thank Ray for coming to his rescue. He and his father had travelled to Dublin on the day of the match with just one ticket for the Davin Stand; they were desperately hoping to swap this for a Hill 16 ticket and then buy a second ticket for the Hill so they could be together.

At 2.30 p.m., just an hour before throw-in, TJ's dad decided that their efforts to secure the tickets had been in vain and they walked towards the North Circular Road hoping to sell their ticket. After meeting with his aunt and uncle, who had a ticket for the Cusack Stand and the Hogan Stand, TJ recalled they stood in the middle of the road trying to sell the ticket. The ticket was almost sold to a woman, but when she saw how distraught TJ was she said she didn't feel right buying the ticket.

As it got even closer to throw-in time, all hope seemed to be lost when, as TJ explained, 'a stranger saw I was upset and asked me if I was okay. My auntie explained that there were four of us and we had three tickets for three different areas of the stadium.' The man said, 'I am from Leitrim and I can't see this young fellow miss seeing his team on All-Ireland Sunday. I will watch the match on the TV and give you my Cusack ticket.'

Expressing his gratitude to Ray Gilmartin for his generous act, TJ said, 'When I am older I hope I can make some young boy as happy as he made me. I think his community should know what a nice thing he did for me.

'We didn't win the match but I will never forget my day in Croke Park.'

FROM HERE TO EQUINITY

A FUNDRAISER WITH a difference was launched on Valentine's Day at the Maxi Zoo pet store in Longford. At the special event, Tiny Tim, a Falabella miniature horse, proposed to his sweetheart, Teany, the smallest pony in Ireland, with an engagement ring. She didn't say 'neigh' and the wedding is set to go ahead.

Tiny Tim has risen to fame in recent years following appearances on the 'Late Late Show' and at the opening ceremony of the Special Olympics, while he also entertains visitors at the National Stud.

Word got out last week that Tiny Tim was about to get down on bended knees, but the couple were tight-lipped. When Patrick Conboy of the *Longford Leader* approached them at their field in Longford, Teany ran to the safety of a waiting bush, while Tiny Tim snorted at journalists when it became apparent no sugar cubes were on offer. However, sources close to the couple say they are keen to start a family, but want to tie the knot first and avoid 'putting the cart before the horse'.

Friends of Tiny Tim – a hopeless romantic – believe he could pop the question by paraphrasing a line from Shakespeare, 'Shall I compare thee to summer hay, thou art more lovely and more tasty ...'

The wedding reception will involve a marquee and live music, but it's understood burgers are off the menu for guests. Insiders are also speculating on the pair's honeymoon destination, with the Curragh, Dubai and Kentucky all believed to be on their shortlist. But no matter where the newly-weds decide to spend their vacation, it is rumoured they will insist on staying in the bridle suite.

CARLOW WOMAN FINISHES WORLD'S BIGGEST JIGSAW

ONE HUNDRED HOURS of painstakingly piecing together the world's largest-ever jigsaw – but an amazing 32,256 pieces later and Ann Doyle has done it! Ann, from Steeple View Crescent, Tullow, completed the gigantic jigsaw in the Dome, Graiguecullen on Wednesday. It was 'a fantastic achievement that very few people in the world have accomplished'.

'It took 100 hours to complete it,' said Ann, who, when asked if it was difficult, replied, 'Ah, no, no jigsaw is a problem to me.

'The bigger the better and the harder the better ... I wouldn't get frustrated one bit. I just love them.'

Ann admits she did have pains in her hands, her neck and her back as, piece by piece, she put the huge jigsaw together and then stuck it down, before mounting it onto a wall at the Dome. The Graiguecullen amusement centre kindly gave Ann the space to make the gigantic jigsaw, which measures an incredible 17 feet long. The jigsaw, which is internationally recognised as the world's largest, is based on the work of artist Keith Haring. Ann sorted out all the edges and the colours first. That alone took two hours, and then she started making it in rows, with 288 pieces on each row.

On Monday Ann's brother-in-law Seán and her husband Paddy framed the jigsaw and placed it on the wall in the Dome, where it will be a permanent reminder of Ann's great work.

Winner's medal returned – 102 years later

A NINE-CARAT GOLD Westmeath Football Championship medal has turned up in the medal box of a famous Galway footballer who had never donned the 'other' maroon.

The story began when Ballinasloe man Cyril Dunne – who himself has won three All-Ireland and six Connaught titles with Galway – brought a box of his equally legendary father's medals to a jeweller's to be cleaned, and up popped this mysterious Westmeath Medal from 1909. Cyril's father was the famous John 'Tull' Dunne, Galway captain in the 1930s. Cyril brought the medal to a school principal in Creagh, who in turn passed it on to a teacher who just happened to be researching Westmeath GAA history.

A search led them to another Dunne family in Monksland, Athlone, the family of the late Joseph Dunne. His son, 90-year-old Bill Dunne, was over the moon to be reunited with his father's medal. It turned out that the men were cousins who hadn't seen each other for many years, but the mystery continued as they found out that Joseph played for Ballinasloe, so it is not known how or why he lined out for Athlone on the fateful day he picked up his Westmeath medal.

EXERCISE CAN GET YOUR GOAT

IT WAS A GRUFF workout for two goats who tried to kid their way into getting free gym membership at Curves, in Ennis, according to Carol Byrne in the *Clare Champion*. On Saturday, the two goats showed they weren't afraid of exercise, having climbed the 20-step staircase to the gym at West Gate Business Park, but after they saw what the action was like in Curves, they weren't prepared to leave in a hurry.

Claudia Nicholson was working when the two goats arrived in for a look-around. 'It was heart-warming and it made all our days. It was a nice situation even though the exercise extended to a bit of a clean-up afterwards,' she said.

The two goats weren't kidding around – they seemed intent on getting in some exercise, having already paid a visit to the P&M Golf Superstore before deciding on Curves.

'They were wandering around the business park on Saturday morning, they went into the golf shop and people there thought they were seeing things. When I arrived at Curves for work ... some of the members said to me, there's someone to see me. They had come upstairs and made themselves comfortable ... they walked into the gym, walking in on seven or eight ladies who were using the gym. They let loose. One of them was fond of an exercise mat and had a pee. It was all a bit of fun,' Claudia recalled.

Claudia said they were only curious about what the gym had to offer and were very friendly, but they did frighten the ladies in the beginning. 'We were petting them. Never had anything like that happened: the most might have been a dog wandering up but nothing like that,' Claudia concluded.

Clare's dog warden, Frankie Coote, explained the two goats were removed having liaised with the Department of Agriculture, and as the animals were untagged and have not been claimed, they have been rehomed.

SPEEDING KERRYMAN GETS BELATED WEDDING PRESENT – FROM A CORK JUDGE

A KILLARNEY MAN appeared in Macroom District Court charged with not paying a fine for a speeding offence recorded by a speed detection van on the N22 at Inchirahilly, Crookstown, on 9 May last. Judge James McNulty noted that the man had missed a prior court appearance for the offence, to which the defendant explained that he was on his honeymoon at the time. He apologised for missing the deadline for paying the fine.

'Well, I daresay you didn't have the right balance of mind at the time; you were pre-occupied with other things. I'll give you a wedding present and spare you the conviction,' Judge McNulty said. Judge McNulty struck out the charge on condition that the defendant pay €100 to the court charity box.

Sex toys used at St Patrick's Day fundraiser

AN ANN SUMMERS PARTY, which included a presentation of sex toys and lingerie along with raunchy party games, was held in Kavanagh's Bar in Portlaoise on Friday evening in aid of the Portlaoise St Patrick's Day Festival.

The party was part of a fake hen party fundraiser for the parade in honour of Ireland's patron saint. The chairperson of the Portlaoise St Patrick's Day committee, Ger Whelan, condemned the event, claiming it was done without his knowledge despite him being 'on the door'. He found out when several revellers expressed their concern to him about what was taking place inside.

'It was something I did not know about. It was added at the last minute. It was stopped after less than 30 minutes,' he said. The fundraising night proceeded normally afterwards.

When asked whether it was appropriate for a sex-themed fundraiser to be associated with a family day out such as St Patrick's Day, Mr Whelan said, 'It's not appropriate. It was supposed to be a bit of fun and a laugh to raise a bit of money. It was not meant to offend anyone or hurt anyone.

'The St Patrick's Day committee want absolutely nothing to do with it. It's something that should not have happened. It was completely inappropriate,' he said. A rogue committee member who had not consulted with the rest of the committee is being blamed.

NOT BEING

'DISADVANTAGED'

IS A HUGE

DISADVANTAGE

FRANK HAS OLDEST WORKING TELEVISION SET IN IRELAND!

Like most sports fans, Ballintubber man Frank Cuffe is planning to watch the London Olympics this summer. However, Frank will tune into the Games on a 64-year-old television set, which has won a prize for being the oldest working television set in Ireland!

Frank Cuffe worked for years as a television repairman and is an avid television collector, who enjoys nothing more than returning an antique television to its former glory. But this hobby of Frank's paid off after he won a competition on Today FM for owning the oldest working television in Ireland with his own EKO black-and-white television, a 1948 EK Cole TSC91.

'I heard about it on the radio and certainly thought that I would be in with a chance to make the top 10 oldest working televisions in the country. But I was thrilled to win it. I sent them in a few images of the television and it obviously was the oldest! I bought it a few years ago from another enthusiast. There aren't too many collectors of old televisions in Ireland, but I have noticed online that there are some in the UK,' he said.

He outdid the owners of 200 vintage televisions, mostly from the 1970s and 1980s, who were invited to send in images and descriptions of their retro sets as part of the Department of Communications' digital switchover awareness campaign. Older than RTÉ itself, Frank's television is working well, in its pride of place in the sitting room of his home.

Married to Carmel, the 43-year-old travelled to Dublin last week to meet host Ray D'Arcy and show off his prized possession. Despite receiving a new Saorview-ready TV valued at €500 for winning the competition, Frank plans to watch the Games on his old-school model which still uses glass valves.

Ironically, the Games were first televised in 1948, the same year that his now award-winning television was made. 'There will really be no difference except it will be black and white. I find that the new televisions can be a bit gimmicky. Granted, there is no HD on the 1948 model, but it still works fine,' joked Frank.

Judge says boy can have a new bike – if he behaves 'till December'

A YOUTH WHO had breached a court-imposed curfew and found himself before Judge Seamus Hughes at Mullingar District Court asked the Judge for another chance. The Judge asked the youth if he had a bicycle. Bemused, he said he did not. 'And would you like one?' the Judge continued. Even more bewildered the child replied that he would.

Judge Hughes then said if the youth behaves himself between now and his next court appearance in December, he will direct Gardaí to spend €400 from the court poor box to buy him a bike and a helmet. 'I don't want a helmet,' said the boy, to grins from the crowd present in court. Of course, the Judge said he must wear his helmet.

'I know what boys are like with bikes,' the Judge declared. As the boy left court, a Garda reminded him to have manners. 'Thanks, Judge,' he said, turning to go. Outside the courtroom, upon hearing of the bike offer, a youth said, 'He should've asked him for an X-Box!'

FUNGIE TAKES COVER AS BIG BROTHERS TRY TO MUSCLE IN

THOSE WHO VENTURED out to Dingle Harbour to see Fungie the Dolphin on Wednesday were surprised to find four bottle-nosed dolphins – but no sign of the star of Dingle Harbour, who embarked on some hide and seek until his finned compatriots left the area.

According to Jeannine Masset, who along with Rudi Schmart photographs and documents Fungie's movements on a daily basis, he was so displeased with the presence of the four strange dolphins that he did something of a disappearing act and even when found wouldn't be coaxed out of his quarters. 'We were surprised when, instead of Fungie, four dolphins popped up beside us last Wednesday,' Jeannine told *The Kerryman*.

'We thought they were friends or family members of Fungie who have been coming for over 20 years and with whom we have had many encounters. These dolphins are usually welcomed by Fungie and he totally interacts with them.'

Jeannine and Rudi have kept records of the various other dolphins who visit Fungie by identifying them by their dorsal fins. 'We found out that the same dolphins have been coming back for so many years that are friendly with Fungie; the last ones that came were a mother and calf in 2011. She also came with a calf in 2010 and she is very friendly with Fungie,' she said. 'Fungie was great with her calf, we watched them for many hours and the calf was copying Fungie in all his movements.'

But Fungie was having none of it when the four strangers showed up in his playground in Dingle Harbour. 'The four that were here were definitely strangers; Fungie did not interact with them and he stayed hidden for hours, we eventually noticed him hiding at a spot where a little stream drops into the sea,' said Jeannine. Later on in the evening, the four visiting dolphins headed for Inch Beach and despite efforts to coax Fungie out of his hidey-hole, the big man wasn't budging.

'There was a reason for this we learned later on as the four dolphins returned for another tour of the harbour; he must have known,' said Jeannine. 'For whatever reason, it was clear that these four dolphins were no friends of Fungie.'

Six thousand coins? No, thanks!

A YOUNG DRIVER was gutted when he was fined for having no tax on his car – while he was at the Motor Tax Office in Tralee. So Daniel Farrell from Keel decided to get his own back by paying the €60 fine in six thousand one-cent coins.

However, the young Kerry man is wondering what to do with six thousand one-cent coins after Tralee Town Council refused the coin as payment for a €60 fine.

Daniel Farrell received the fine while parked in the Brandon car park in Tralee as he walked to the council office to pay his motor tax. Acknowledging he was in the wrong but frustrated that he had tried to pay the tax, Daniel decided to pay the €60 fine in one-cent coins. However, his jest backfired as legally the town council could not accept it, and he is now left with the spare change.

Ram a lamb a ding dong!

A lamb bred and reared on a farm in County Laois has shattered records across the pond, after being sold for a staggering €107,582 (£94,000 sterling) at a Scottish market. The Suffolk ram lamb earned an eye-watering sum for his owner Dan Tynan, from Ardlea just outside Colt, County Laois. This was an outstanding entry into pedigree-bred lamb sales for Laois vendor Tynan, as he only started his own flock last year.

The astonishing sale took place at the breed society's Stirling meet in Scotland. Welshman Myfyr Evans was the proud winning bidder for the Laois lamb, who is yet to be named. Myfyr's huge bid shattered the breed record for a Suffolk sheep, which previously stood at 75,000 guineas.

The Welsh farmer spotted the Ardlea flock ram lamb during a day trip to Ireland just over a month ago. After travelling over on ferry from Holyhead to visit an agricultural show in Kilkenny but seeing nothing of interest, Myfyr dropped in to Dan Tynan's farm, where the Ardlea lamp caught his eye. Speaking to the *Daily Post* newspaper in Wales, Myfyr said that the Laois lamb is 'the best' he had seen in a long time.

'He has style and colour; he is long and powerful, with a good top line. He's got everything. And so he should have, at that price.' Myfyr sees Wales's most expensive lamb as a sound investment rather than an impulse buy.

Tophill Joe, a different breed of ram, which broke records of its own in 2004, went on to earn £1 million and sire more than 1,000 lambs.

TIME TRAVELLING IN KERRY

TIME AND TIDE stand still for no man but Valentia Islander Patrick Curtin discovered this month that his island home seemed to be falling behind the rest of the world by several minutes every day. The retired boat-builder observed that Valentia was fast becoming a 'lost kingdom' by literally watching his electric clocks lose up to 23 minutes in a week.

'I have a clock radio at my bedside and it displays the time,' Patrick explained. 'One morning, I discovered the beeps were going off at 6 a.m. on the radio but the clock display was behind. The next morning, I noticed it was three minutes slow again.'

A small battery-operated travel clock seemed to be keeping perfect time, however. Patrick decided to conduct an experiment by monitoring the electric clock on his cooker in the kitchen. After seven days, the clock was 23 minutes slow. 'I was asking a few people and they said their clocks were a bit funny as well,' he said.

'I rang Radio Kerry and went on air. Lo and behold, the whole of south Kerry were ringing in saying their clocks were gone "cuckoo" or away with the fairies.' Not only was the island slipping into a parallel time zone by up to three minutes a night, but also homes all over the Cahersiveen area were falling behind the times.

Patrick sourced the problem to the use of generators by the ESB while maintenance works were being carried out at a power station in Cahersiveen. An ESB spokesman confirmed generators were in use for about three weeks when the Guarranebane Station in Cahersiveen was out for maintenance. The spokesman said the Cahersiveen area and Valentia Island would have been affected.

'The area was being generated for two or three weeks,' the spokesperson confirmed. 'The power would have been the same but there would have been some fluctuations with the generators.'

'To be able to put the clock back is great,' Patrick joked. 'People should be delighted.'

KERRYMAN THOUGHT GARDA STATION WAS B&B

A KERRY MAN who was so drunk he fell asleep in the public area of the garda station, believing it to be a B&B, was ordered to sign a bond promising to keep the peace for two years. At the district court, the man was warned by Judge Catherine Staines that his purpose was 'not to entertain the public', after he played to the crowd when his mobile phone went off in court.

The defendant was charged that on 13 September, the night before his first court sitting, he fell asleep on a bench at 3 a.m. in Portlaoise Garda Station and had to be wakened. He was in a highly intoxicated state and fell to the ground when he tried to get up. 'He said he thought he was in a B&B,' the Inspector said.

Defence, Ms Elaine Dunne, explained that her client had been in Portlaoise to attend his court date the next morning and he couldn't get a bed and breakfast to stay in. 'He thought he could stay in the garda station,' Ms Dunne said.

'Do you accept you have a drink problem?' Judge Staines asked the defendant.

'I do indeed,' he replied.

'And what are you doing about it?' she asked.

'Drinking more,' he said.

The man was ordered to sign a peace bond, and he must attend alcohol treatment and abstain from drink.

Meathmen thought Garda's car was a taxi

TWO MEATHMEN HAD a few drinks too many and thought they were boarding a cab, but it turned out to be the private car of Garda Patrick Lynott. Instead of going home, their destination was Kells District Court which heard they sat in the back and started 'giving directions to the Garda to bring them home'. Judge Patrick McMahon asked, 'Is there something in the water around Meath,' before telling both men a charity donation or a fine awaited them.

REWARD OFFERED
FOR MISSING HEAD

IT HAS BEEN a permanent fixture putting a smile on passers-by in the Lissivigeen area for over a decade, but poor 'Timber Man' has quite literally lost his head.

Pride and joy of local residents Pat and Deborah O'Keeffe, the quirky wooden figure by the side of the Cork Road has been dressed up in all sorts of guises down through the years, from Santa Claus to Frankenstein and more. Killjoys, though, seem to have taken exception when they unceremoniously decapitated Timber Man to the dismay of the local homeowners who have offered a reward for its return.

'We're pretty annoyed to be honest,' Deborah told the *Kerryman*. 'It's not the first time this has been attempted and we've caught people in recent months trying this under darkness. We knew it was only a matter of time before they got away with it and they struck when we were out at a 50th birthday party.

'We are offering a reward of a tiny timber man to anyone who can give us information leading to the recovery of the head.'

Made out of ESB poles discarded after the electricity board updated the grid, the figure has become a landmark in the area, and was the pride and joy of carpenter Pat who also made a similar figure in the Maherees area. Deborah regularly dresses him up for various occasions and people would stop to have their picture taken with him.

Doused in creosote to preserve the wood, Deborah believes the lost head may have been taken by car by pranksters but it may not have travelled too far as the fumes would have been pretty strong. 'We are sure that whoever took it probably dumped it on the side of the road. We are hoping that someone will find it and return it to us. This Halloween we may have to dress him as the headless horseman,' she added with a smile.

Follow the Yellow Sick Road ...

EXASPERATED RESIDENTS IN Belmullet have painted the hundreds of potholes that pock-mark their area bright yellow, in order to draw attention to the problem. Motorists can now follow the Yellow Sick Road.

The road, leading to the Seaside and Cuan Oisrí estates and the Shore Road, was already in disrepair before the freezing weather conditions during December and January led to a further deterioration of road conditions. The surface is now so potholed that locals have had enough.

Resident and estate agent Derek Reilly has highlighted the holes in the road with bright yellow paint. 'The road was never in a great state but in the last four months it has really gone to the dogs. It's like an unfinished jigsaw,' said Mr Reilly, who is the current president of Erris Chamber of Commerce.

He has lost count of the number of times Mayo County Council has been alerted to the problem. He claims the local authority has poured chipping into the potholes but it hasn't worked and residents are sick of stop-gap measures.

'I don't understand why they don't just do a right job on it. It's a disgrace,' said Mr Reilly, who was inspired to paint the potholes by a campaigner in County Cavan. 'There's a man in Cavan who has done this before. He travels around actively seeking out areas that have pothole problems.'

Cavan man Martin Hannigan, aged 54, used luminous paint to warn motorists of the potholes from 1998 until he agreed to give up his actions after appearing before Cootehill District Court in September 2009. Locals in Belmullet hope that the yellow markings will force the Council to finally take action and fix their road.

Earlier this year, Mayo County Council admitted there was a 'plague of potholes' on the county's roads. A study by AA Ireland revealed that Mayo is one of the worst counties in Ireland for potholes. AA asked respondents to name the last time they hit a pothole that necessitated a garage repair or a call-out to the AA. In the first three months of 2011, a staggering 21.1 per cent of drivers in County Mayo reported damaging their vehicle or requiring a call-out.

COUNTY LIMERICK CEMETERY 'A DEATH TRAP'

A west Limerick cemetery which is due to be enlarged has been described as 'a death trap' by a local county councillor, who feels that serious traffic problems there have been completely ignored. Limerick County Council is to press ahead with a planned two-acre extension to the Reilig Mhuire burial ground near Askeaton, which is located on the main N69 in a 100 kmph speed limit zone.

However, local Councillor Kevin Sheahan has criticised the fact that no efforts are to be taken to tackle 'extremely dangerous' traffic problems at the site, namely the parking of dozens of cars along the main road whenever funerals are taking place.

The Council has insisted that 'there is no record of any collision or safety problems' at the graveyard, and the extension will not exacerbate the parking situation. However, Councillor Sheahan said that the road approaching the cemetery is 'a death trap', and parked cars can cause significant problems on funeral days, particularly for heavy goods traffic heading to and from Foynes Port. 'It's extremely dangerous, and that's not a word I use lightly. I dread the thought of what could happen there some day.'

Begorrah! Bandon has the most leprechauns in Ireland

THE TOWN OF BANDON was 'a field of green' on St Patrick's Day as its citizens, supported by friends from its hinterland and as far away as the UK, Spain and Haiti, took centre stage in a bid to break the Guinness World Record for leprechauns as part of the St Patrick's Day celebrations.

Following another fantastic parade through the town, an amazing 1,263 green men and women of every shape, size and age packed the middle of South Main Street, to beat the total of 1,124 set earlier that day by leprechauns in Glenties, County Donegal, and way ahead of the previous record of 414 by a school in South Africa last year.

It was a remarkable achievement by a dynamic team led by Ger Fitzgerald, who had been working flat out over the past few weeks, at sweat shops in the hotel and other venues, making the leprechaun outfits comprising a waistcoat, top hat, black trousers, buckle and beard, all of which had to comply with the strict rules of the Guinness World Records inspectors who will confirm the valid final tally in a few weeks' time.

Declan Crowley was the hard working MC for the parade and leprechauns were registered by Ann Doyle, Theresa McCarthy and Jacinta Warren. All were then counted by Phil Murphy and Councillor Andrew Coleman, after which all 1,263 had to stay in the same place for ten minutes, before Andrew sounded the siren to loud cheers of delight in what was a carnival atmosphere, and sang 'Ireland's Call'.

Special awards were presented to leprechauns: youngest, Cillian O'Donovan–O'Donoghue (two weeks); oldest, Mary McLernon (80 years); tallest, Alan O'Mahony (6'5"); shiniest buckle, Albert O'Donoghue; and leprechaun who travelled the furthest, Prospery Raymond from Haiti. There was great support from Gerry Fitzgerald and members of Bandon Co-Marketing Group, Trevor Collins and members of Bandon Working Together, and various local clubs.

WE'RE THROWING MONEY IN THE RIVER – AND WE'VE BEEN DOING IT FOR YEARS, DIVERS DISCOVER

THERE'S MONEY IN that there river! Old coins have a habit of turning up in the place where you least expect them to, such as old buildings, buried in gardens or the glovebox of the car.

However, as members of the Blackwater Sub Aqua Club will readily testify, our rivers and waterways can also prove to be fertile hunting grounds for numismatists (coin collectors). Blackwater SAC spokesman Timmy Carey said many people are unaware of just how regularly divers come across coins buried in silt on riverbeds.

'While the bulk of these tend to be recent coins of small denomination, occasionally, when the mud is cleaned away, you may find you have a rare coin on your hands,' said Timmy. 'These can include coins from all over the world. Our divers have found rare French francs, a German token and even a World War I vintage penny,' he added.

Only last year divers in Fermoy found a Welsh coin which was at least 200 years old and now sits proudly among the exhibits at the National Museum in Dublin.

Timmy said there are still vast quantities of our waterways that have never been explored, 'so who knows what still may lay hidden below their surfaces,' he said. 'That was highlighted by the recent find of a very rare special Viking sword in the river Shannon by the Shannonside Sub Aqua Club.'

Timmy said that just as mystifying, given the current economic times, was the amount of new coins that divers find in the Blackwater. 'One of our divers recently surfaced with the princely sum of 11 euro coins. It is strange that people throw their money into the river, given that we are in the midst of a recession,' he said. 'Mind you in 200 years' time some of these coins could create a stir of excitement themselves,' laughed Timmy.

BRAVEHEART TO TACKLE THE DUMPERS?

A SIGN BEARING the words 'Brave Heart?' has begun appearing at illegal dumping sites. A declaration of war against fly-tippers or a further affront by those dumping along the side of the road, the Braveheart mystery is confounding residents in south Armagh. Ever since its appearance, mounted in the midst of rubbish dumped on the roadside on the rural Captains Road outside Forkhill a few weeks ago, the 'Brave Heart?' sign has confused residents.

'While this is sadly not the first time this spot has been used by dumpers, it is really perplexing this time,' one resident told the *Newry Reporter*. 'What does it mean?'

The most likely allusion is to Mel Gibson's big budget William Wallace epic of the same name, but the lack of a fly-tipping story strand to the plot does leave everyone, barring the person or persons who planted it there, at a loss. Is it an allegory, perhaps declaring war on those who are depositing their waste at the beauty spot? A warning perhaps that a Scottish warrior is preparing to defend the lands?

Slieve Gullion Councillor Anthony Flynn is as bemused as everyone else. 'I haven't a clue who put the sign there or what it's supposed to mean, but I've informed the Council's Environmental Health department and all this rubbish will be removed soon,' the Councillor said. 'Due to the proximity to the border, we've speculated it could be fly-tipping from outside the district, but whoever is leaving this rubbish here is destroying our beautiful countryside and I urge them to stop.'

With William Wallace potentially watching, perhaps this would be for the best.

Wrigley's believe it or not: Trim looks to ban gum!

A STICKY SITUATION may await Trim Town Council if it proceeds with proposals to ask local shopkeepers to stop selling chewing gum. At January's monthly council meeting, councillors basking in the afterglow of the recent Irish Business Against Litter (IBAL) victory, proclaiming Trim as the country's cleanest town, heard Councillor Gerry Reilly put forward the idea that shopkeepers in the town be asked not to sell chewing gum because of it sticking to paths and the expense involved in removing it.

Councillor Reilly said that his inspiration came from a recent trip to Singapore, where he noted the lack of litter on streets in the city. He told councillors that so strict were Singaporean laws that it was 'three lashes or a couple of days [in jail]' for minor offences like littering. He also noted 'nobody blows their horns at each other' and 'there's no chewing gum anywhere, no plastic bags, or it's three lashes'.

He added, 'Now, I'm not saying we bring that [lashes] in ... but we should have a look at being the first town in Ireland to be chewing gum-free. Think about it, Trim being the first town in Ireland with no chewing gum. We would probably be the first town in the EU [to do it].'

Town Clerk Brian Murphy said the idea had 'merits' and that he would look into it as councillors warmed to the proposal. However, the *Meath Chronicle* spoke to local shop-owners in the town this week and found that unanimous disagreement would be registered against any move.

POSTMEN PUSHING THEIR LUCK AT CHRISTMAS

AMONG MANY TALES by Mike Hackett is a great yarn about a postman in the area back in the 1930s who used to be the most popular man at Christmas because many of the locals who could not read or write depended on him to read out Christmas cards or letters from exiled sons and daughters in England and America. Well, he used to invent the last line of every Christmas letter as 'don't forget to stand to the poor postman for Christmas', i.e. give him a few bob.

In the 1950s the same man got two helpers to help him deliver parcels to homes in the suburbs and countryside. He would stay in the van whilst the others ran up and down the drives delivering the goods. One woman was so excited by a parcel that she stood the postman's apprentice a fiver – a huge stand at the time.

But he decided to push his luck a bit further: 'Thank you, ma'am, but there are three of us and what is five divided by three?' He was being the cute fool – fishing for another pound. 'Oh, I'm sorry,' said the woman. 'One moment please ...' She soon appeared with three single pound notes! 'Now, my dear man, happy Christmas to the three of you,' said she, taking back the fiver.

Woman fined for driving with onion ring

A WOMAN SPOTTED eating while driving wound up with a fine of €200 when she was convicted of driving without reasonable consideration at Mullingar District Court. Asked by Judge Seamus Hughes what she was eating, the defendant said it was an onion ring. The alleged offence took place on 29 March at Portnashangan.

JACK THE RIPPER FROM CAVAN? OH YES HE IS, OH NO HE'S NOT ...

A SO-CALLED 'RIPPEROLOGIST' allegedly traced the infamous London serial killer Jack the Ripper to Cavan. Jack the Ripper killed 11 women in the East End of London between 1888 and 1891; he was never caught and it is one of the greatest whodunnit cases in history. But Irish crime profiler Siobhán Patricia Mulcahy claims to have cracked it.

Mulcahy followed a trail of information, local legend and recollections of an old woman from Kerry relating to Irish-born Francis Tumblety, who many believe to be one of the chief suspects. He was traced right back to the town of Killycollie, now known as Bailieborough. Records show that his parents James and Margaret Tumblety were from there, and they had 11 children. And in one of Tumblety's autobiographies, he describes visiting 'Inniskillen Falls' in 1882, today better known as Tullydermot Falls.

But this week, a letter to the editor refutes those findings and says Jack the Ripper was not from Bailieborough:

Dear Editor,
Your 'Jack the Ripper' article by 'Ripperologist' Siobhán Patricia Mulcahy in this week's Anglo-Celt *claiming that the infamous 'Jack the Ripper's' parents came from Bailieborough did not go down well over here around Bailieborough. Now we are not blaming Siobhán, because she was conned by that 'Cavan woman' who gave her the information but would not give her own name.*

When I was very young, which is a very long time ago, our farmhouse was what was then known as a 'Céilidh House'

where old men came at night and sitting around the big open hearth fire discussed the local, national and international news (which they heard on Radio Éireann). I was a 'nosy' child and my bedroom was next to the kitchen and I used to listen behind the door when they thought I was asleep and Jack the Ripper was discussed nearly every night. Not only because of those horrible crimes but also because a man from away below the town (Bailieborough) was supposed to be him. The James Tumulty, a prime suspect in those 11 dreadful murders, had no connection whatsoever with the town of Bailieborough or this area.

According to those old people who were around in the 1880/90s, the Bailieborough connection came about when a young local man, who was 'hired' (contracted to work for and live with a farming family for six months) became too friendly with the farmer's daughter and like many young inquisitive teenagers before the internet they began exploring and experimenting in the mysterious and forbidden land of the big S. Unfortunately one of their experiments went wrong and the girl became pregnant. The farmer was naturally not pleased with this development and went for his double-barrelled shotgun, and the farmhand went for his bicycle and the boat to England.

The pregnant girl was in love with the boy and wanted to go to England to him but her mother, a right old rip by all accounts, was dead against that and began to spread bad stories about the lad. Around about that time the news of the terrible murders in London broke and the hunt was on for 'Jack the Ripper', as they called the notorious serial killer, and the old doll spread the story that the murderer was in fact their former 'servant boy' who 'had raped her daughter and got her pregnant and skipped off to England'.

The rest as they say is history.

Yours,
Peter McConnell
Bailieborough

Megalithic tomb at home in estate

IT'S NOT WHAT you would expect to find in the middle of a housing estate, but Garavogue Villas is home to a megalithic monument. In the townland of Abbeyquarter North, the historic site can be found at a roundabout. The houses surrounding this site were built in the 1940s and the religious statues were erected on it by local residents to celebrate Holy Year in 1950. They have since become a familiar Sligo landmark.

The boulders surrounding the site are in fact a simple passage tomb, dating back almost 6000 years. It is very similar in size and construction to one of the passage tombs at Carrowmore, just west of Sligo City (Carrowmore tomb 27, which was dated to around 3700 B.C.).

The site consists of 44 boulders with a diameter of 23 metres, some of which are displaced from their original position. It may have had an inner circle and there were four stones recorded in the centre in 1888, with only one being visible today.

Col. William Gregory Wood-Martin, the local landlord and celebrated Sligo antiquarian, excavated it in 1888 and drew a plan of it, with the help of William Wakeman, an illustrator and antiquarian who taught at Portora Royal School in Enniskillen. They found cremated bone and some unburnt bone, including human and animal teeth, some of which belonged to a dog or wolf. The remains might be evidence of the monument being used at different periods through prehistory.

For example, Carrowmore tomb 27 had both Neolithic (*c*. 4000–2400 B.C.) remains and Iron Age (*c*. 500 B.C.–A.D. 400) remains in it, some of which are similar to those found by Wood-Martin, particularly the dog/wolf teeth.

The passage tomb at Abbeyquarter is directly overlooking the narrowest point of the Garavogue River, where the river goes from being 200 m wide to 42.5 m wide. Up until recently this was called Buckley's Ford and was the location of Smyth's Brewery back in the 1820s.

Abbeyquarter's role in the landscape may have functioned as a symbolic marker and could have acted as an aid to direct people toward the ritual centre of the Cúil Irra Peninsula, where the Carrowmore passage tombs and Queen Maeve's cairn are located.

MAN FOUND LYING ON GROUND WITH TROUSERS AROUND ANKLES TRYING TO EAT A BURGER

COCONUTS IN SCHULL SHIPWRECK

UNDERWATER ARCHAEOLOGISTS ARE investigating the wreck of a wooden merchant ship which carried a cargo of coconuts to Ireland in the sixteenth century. It was discovered during pipe works in Schull Harbour. The ship, believed to date back to the sixteenth century, is buried in the seabed in 10 m of water just off the shoreline.

Contracted underwater archaeologist Julianna O'Donoghue immediately suspended pipe-laying works on the multimillion Schull Wastewater Treatment Plant when machines struck and partly damaged the wreck. The ship's cargo of coconuts was uncovered during this process.

Little is known of the wreck's origins at present as archaeologists' work continues. An exclusion zone has been erected around the wreck site and experts are keen to discourage looters from gaining access to any valuable materials on board.

Believed to be a 'sizeable' vessel, the bulk of the wreck is buried in silt with only a small portion exposed. Archaeologists are now working to determine how old it is and what it was doing in Irish waters.

Explorations of the ship are set to continue for some weeks. Because of its cargo of coconuts, it is thought the ship's origins may be linked to the Caribbean. The discovery will be valuable to historians in terms of developing a greater understanding of historical Irish trade links to the 'new world'.

Work on the laying of outfall pipes will resume once an exclusion zone protecting the find is in place.

THE MYSTERIOUS CASE OF THE FADING ECHO AT LOCAL LANDMARK

WHERE HAS THE ECHO GONE? Generations of Trim people recall as youngsters stopping at Trim's Echo Gate for a shout across the Boyne towards the medieval ruins and their delight to hear their voices bounce back. It's a tradition that is not as common as it once was, but is that because the echo just isn't as good as it used to be?

At the monthly meeting of Trim Town Council, Cathaoirleach Councillor James O'Shea raised the matter and said he did not believe the echo was as good as it once was – and that a number of people had said this to him.

He said the Echo Gate was a major local attraction and they should do whatever they can to make a feature of it. 'When I was growing up, there was a great echo,' he said. Councillor Gerry Reilly suggested that perhaps it was because the trees in the area had grown higher and were absorbing the sound more.

Believe it or not, a roar at Echo Gate is rated as the 39th 'Thing to Do' in County Meath on *Lonely Planet*.

EUROMILLIONS WINNER 'MAKES HAY WHEN THE SUN SHINES'

FOR YEARS, BACHELOR Ronnie McDonnell from Knocklore, Ardee, has driven to the Village Shop in Jonesborough, owned by his pal Seamus McNamee, to buy tickets for the EuroMillions draws. And it all paid off when his ticket matched five numbers and one Lucky Star in a recent draw and landed him a whopping £204,490.70.

Ronnie's first purchase was a new John Deere hay baler. 'This couldn't have come at a better time,' said Ronnie. 'I've needed a new baler for some time now but I just couldn't afford it. I'm going to make hay while the sun shines.' Ronnie isn't planning any holidays but a trip to the Listowel Races in September is on the cards for the man who likes a little flutter. 'I'm fairly sensible with my money but maybe I'll have a slightly larger bet than usual.'

'Sod it for a pint' in Keash

PATRONS OF A PUB in Keash didn't have to pay for their pints and spirits on Saturday night – they simply received them in exchange for a bag of turf! The owner of Fox's Den, Patrick Ward, estimated that this night of bartering and swapping pints for turf was good business, given that he now doesn't have to pay to stock up with fuel to keep his two fires burning this winter.

Patrick said the idea for the 'Sod it for a pint' night of swapping pints for turf came from a customer about a year ago. He decided to go ahead with it for one night this year and was thrilled at the crowds it drew to the pub. Customers were limited to four bags of turf in exchange for four drinks, and Patrick said that the novel idea generated a great buzz as more and more people arrived with bags of turf!

'Instead of people talking about doom and gloom, it generated a great atmosphere. It's the start of winter and it creates a good buzz with people. Of course, there's also a more serious side to it. Pubs have changed an awful lot in the past 10 years and country pubs especially have a struggle to keep going,' he commented.

Given the success of the night, Patrick says that he intends to run another similar night next year. 'Maybe we'll look at doing it into the New Year, when we need more turf, but I reckon we've enough here to get us through the winter! It's a hard time for all businesses, pubs included. Everyone in the trade would accept that you've to offer something different to customers and our night was a play on that.'

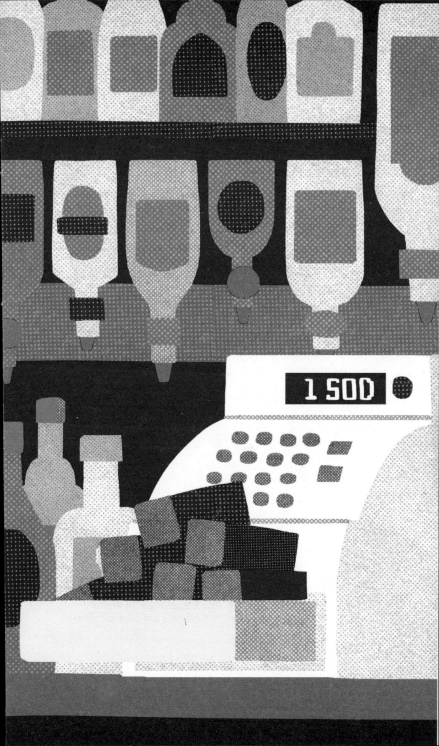

Woman is fined for her 'raucous' singing

IF ONE PARTICULAR TRALEE woman is ever again told to quit singing on a bus, chances are she'll heed the warning, after a drink-fuelled sing-song on a trip from Limerick resulted in a trip to court. The woman appeared at Listowel District Court on Thursday, where her solicitor explained that her singing became 'a bit raucous', resulting in the Gardaí being called. The incident happened on a Bus Éireann bus on 16 October last.

'She was on the bus from Limerick to Tralee with her daughter and had a few drinks on board and started singing,' Solicitor Pat Enright explained. 'Unfortunately, around Listowel the singing got a bit raucous and people couldn't stop her. She's hugely apologetic and embarrassed about the whole thing,' he added. Judge Aeneas McCarthy convicted the defendant of being intoxicated in a public place and fined her €200.

Halfwit burglars cause power cut in Hanover

BUNGLING BURGLARS CUT off power to estates around Hanover in Carlow Town in the early hours of Thursday morning when they attempted to hot-wire the alarm system in Penney's. The culprits, who were trying to cut the alarm cord before breaking into the building, managed to disconnect electricity along Hanover Road in the early-morning botch job.

The gang then tripped the alarm when they broke into Penney's at approximately 4.30 a.m. and were quickly interrupted by Gardaí and the store key holder, who responded to the alarm activation.

Gardaí disturbed a number of intruders in mid-theft, who then fled the scene with a small quantity of cash and clothing. The group sped off out the Hanover exit in the direction of Carlow Town in a silver Toyota Land Cruiser. Several ESB crews were brought in to restore power to the area.

Mayor of Limerick wants Polish street signs

EURO 2012 DID a lot to cement already-strong relations between Ireland and Poland, and in a bid to make non-Irish nationals feel more at home, Limerick Mayor Gerry McLoughlin wants to see the city's street signs in Polish – and, er, 'African'.

At present, all street signs across Ireland are displayed in English, then Irish. But the new mayor wants to see Limerick go a step further – and embrace its sizeable population from Europe and Africa by including further translations.

'I am passionate about bringing everyone together. I was an immigrant myself: I have family abroad still in Wales and Australia so I understand what it is like. We have thousands of Poles and other foreign nationals here,' he explained. 'I would like to see some Polish and African signs going up,' he said in an interview with the *Limerick Leader*. Polish translations for some of the city centre streets include Ulica O'Connell (O'Connell Street), Ulica Rejsy (*Cruise's Street*) and Półksiężyc (the Crescent).

It would not be the first time the Polish language has been thought of for official signage in Ireland: in 2006, Laois County Council sought to include Polish on road signs to reduce the number of fatalities.

THE BLAA JOINS

EUROPE'S 'UPPER

CRUST'!

THE LEGENDARY WATERFORD BLAA – be it floury or crusty – has been successfully registered for prestigious Protected Geographic Indication (PGI) status! This significant development has seen the city's most famed culinary creation earn the same status as internationally renowned products such as Italy's Parma Ham, France's Camembert de Normandie Cheese and Greece's Kalamata Olive Oil.

This special designation was marked at a special celebratory event held at the Waterford Medieval Museum, 'a great news day for Waterford' in the view of Minister for Agriculture Simon Coveney.

So how did this all come about? Back in 2009, a meeting of four traditional family bakeries from County Waterford and south Kilkenny led to the establishment of the Waterford Blaa Bakers' Association. The main objectives of the group, composed of M & D Bakery, Hickey's Bakery, Barron's Bakery and Kilmacow Bakery, were to protect the Waterford Blaa as a traditional Irish food product and to register it as a protected food product in Europe.

And they've done that, placing the Blaa in a new shop window for potentially spectacular sales growth throughout the continent. 'Acquiring PGI designation for the Waterford Blaa will help provide a platform to market and promote the Blaa as a unique regional product of Ireland. PGI status will also provide the product with protection against imitation throughout Europe.'

The Minister added, 'A PGI is a symbol of quality within Europe. This unique quality product is distinguished by the use of simple ingredients, traditional skills and local knowledge to produce something that has become a symbol of Waterford and a much loved food of the Waterford people for generations.'

The story of the Blaa goes back over 300 years to the 1690s, when the French Huguenots arrived in Ireland introducing white flour and their very capable baking skills. Made with no artificial additives or preservatives, the Blaa is shaped into small balls, flattened, proved and sprinkled with white flour before baking. Long may the Blaa reign – throughout Europe!

'FAIC' ALL HAPPENS IN DINGLE
IN THE MORNING, SAYS JUDGE

'FAIC' ALL HAPPENS in Dingle bars at 9 a.m. in the morning! That was the initial opinion of a local district court judge as an application from a local publican for an early-hours licence came before him. Solicitor Marguerite O'Sullivan informed Judge James O'Connor at Dingle District Court on Friday that local publican Tom Geaney was seeking an early-hours licence for his premises, the Dingle Pub, on Main Street.

The licence would allow for the serving of alcohol from as early as 9 a.m., the Court heard. 'What goes on at 9 a.m. in Dingle?' the Judge quizzed, supplying a solution himself in quick succession and much to the mirth of the court: 'There's one Irish word that answers that question – "faic!" Níl "faic" ar siúl!'

'What's so special about it [the Dingle Pub] that it attracts people at that hour of the morning?' he also asked.

Ms O'Sullivan explained that the early-house licence was required for the service of the 'lawful' tourism trade and other custom streams. Superintendent Jim O'Connor informed the Court that the early-hours licence would also be of considerable attraction to the many fishing crews coming back from the sea by night to Dingle Harbour.

The State had no objection to the application, Superintendent O'Connor added. Judge O'Connor duly granted it, ensuring hard-working fishermen and early-bird tourists need never thirst for anything stronger than milk or water early in Dingle again.

BURGLAR MAKES OFF WITH VALUABLE SHIRT

GARDAÍ IN CARNEW are looking for a snappily dressed burglar who has a keen eye for men's fashion, following a break-in to a house on Sunday afternoon. Shocked householders at Mill Lane, Carnew, returned home on Sunday evening at 7 p.m. to find their front door had been burst open and the house burgled.

Various drawers throughout the house were rifled through, but, bizarrely, all they could determine missing was a shirt. This was no ordinary shirt, though. This was a top quality, high-value Tommy Hilfiger branded shirt. Though the exact size of the missing shirt isn't available, it was described as having navy and blue stripes.

Gardaí also suspect that a burglary near Kilegan on the same afternoon may be linked and have asked anyone with information to contact Carnew Gardaí.

DRIVER MISSED CHECKPOINT THAT COULD HAVE BEEN SEEN FROM OUTER SPACE

A GARDA CHECKPOINT which 'could have been seen from outer space' was somehow not seen by a passing local driver. A man before Tuam Court claimed he missed a Garda in a high visibility vest, with his torch on and his patrol car flashing its blue lights and siren. Judge Geoffrey Browne reckoned it could have been seen from outer space, and he convicted and fined the driver €200 for failing to stop at the garda checkpoint, which was located outside Tuam on the night of 15 November last.

When defence solicitor Danny McGrath asked prosecuting Garda Alan Sheeran what possible motive his client could have for pretending not to see his checkpoint, the Garda replied 'maybe because he had no tax on the car'.

Garda Sheeran said he was manning a checkpoint on the Milltown Road on 15 November last at approximately 8.30 in the evening. It was dark and his patrol car was in the middle of the road with its blue lights flashing and he had all his high visibility safety gear on. He saw the man approach who indicated as if he intended to obey his signal to pull in, but instead he drove on to the hard shoulder and failed to stop.

The defendant insisted he had not seen the checkpoint and was unaware the Garda wanted him to stop. He was surprised when the patrol car stopped him but denied he was trying to avoid detection because he had no tax on his car. 'So you were smack bang in the middle of the road with the blue lights you could see from outer space and he says he couldn't see you. Maybe the road's too good,' the Judge put to Garda Sheeran.

He said he passed by the patrol car at about 40–50 mph. 'You passed through a garda checkpoint at that speed and, worse, you say you didn't even see it.'

'You had no tax and you thought you'd take a chance,' Insp. Michael O'Dwyer put to him. Judge Browne convicted him on both charges and imposed fines totalling €200.

Cromwell and King Billy sought after Charleville raid

OLIVER CROMWELL AND William of Orange are being sought by Gardaí in Charleville following a theft outside the town in the early hours of Tuesday morning. Busts of the pair have been stolen from a gate lodge near Milltown Cross. The busts date from the seventeenth century and were said to be 'an expression of allegiance' of the castle's former occupants. Despite their controversial roles in Irish history, Cromwell and King Billy had survived relatively unscathed for three centuries – although Cromwell's nose was claimed as a prize, probably by the IRA, in 1921.

GALWAY MAN HIRES OUT SPECIAL FUNERAL BOUNCY CASTLES

A GALWAY BUSINESSMAN has hit upon the novel idea of renting out a bouncy castle to entertain children at a funeral, while all the adults continue mourning in the house. Kenneth Gilhooly has already provided the bespoke black bouncy castle service at eight funerals this summer. Apart from the more morbid colour, the bouncy castle looks the same as the standard one. It has a layer of fine Nylcro netting which 'acts as sort of light soundproofing to keep down the noise of children playing in it'.

Specially made to order in Hungary, Kenneth says, 'Obviously, the booking of them is more express than would be the case with a communion or a christening, but we come in and erect the castle discreetly so that we do not offend any people's sensibilities'. Demand is so strong Kenneth hopes to be operating a dozen funeral castles before the end of the year.

MAN WANTED LIFT
HOME IN AMBULANCE

A MAN WHO had missed the last bus from Mayo claimed he had chest pain in order to get an ambulance to bring him home to Roscommon, a GP has revealed. Dr Ken Egan, a family doctor in Ballindine, County Mayo, said the case was among a growing number he was encountering where people were abusing the health service.

The man missed the bus from Mayo to Roscommon and hoped to get there in an ambulance. 'I got the call from the man complaining of chest pain. I said he should go to the hospital in Castlebar but he said he wanted to be taken to Roscommon. I said that is not possible, you are in Mayo,' Dr Egan told the annual meeting of the Irish Medical Organisation (IMO).

'It turned out he had missed the last bus to Roscommon and was going to get home by ambulance. He went to the hospital in Castlebar and was discharged at 2 a.m., when he demanded a taxi to return to Roscommon.'

Dr Egan called for a charge to be imposed on medical-card holders who contacted doctors in the evening and at night to discourage abuse of the system. But his proposal to charge was not supported by other family doctors at the meeting, who said it would affect genuinely vulnerable patients and that the IMO was already opposed to the prescription charge for medical-card holders.

RECYCLE YOUR DEAD IN NOVEL NORTHERN IRELAND CEMETERY

A ROAD SIGN pointing towards a cemetery in County Down has been changed following complaints that it was in bad taste. The same sign, put up by Ards Borough Council, also directed motorists to a new recycling facility outside Comber.

The issue was raised by a Stormont assembly member, who took grave offence at the sign, complaining that combining the two facilities on a single sign was 'highly inappropriate'. The council later apologised 'for any upset the error has caused'. It promised that 'more sensitive signage' would be put up. While both facilities are on adjoining sites, the new directions are erected on the same posts but on separate signs.

UK Independence Party assembly member David McNarry said he was pleased that the sign had been changed. 'I think the council have acted responsibly and fair play to them – it was totally insensitive,' he said. 'A couple of wags had been saying, "If they don't bury you, they'll recycle you," but people were sensitive about it.

'It was something that just needed a bit more care and attention – somebody just didn't think, but it's important to have respect.'

PHEW PHEW — TRAIN STOPS JUST IN TIME AS DRIVER SMASHES CAR THROUGH BARRIERS AFTER CHASE

Imagine! John Lennon's mic turns up in rural Longford

The microphone John Lennon used when he recorded *Imagine* has turned up in rural Longford.

The Live Transmission Studios in the village of Drumlish is the new home of the famous mic, which was bought by Mullingar band the Aftermath. The microphone, which has not been switched on since 1971, fetched over €7,000 at an auction and the band plan to use it on their new album.

Lennon had installed the microphone in his Georgian manor estate Tittenhurst Park near Ascot in 1970, and the location went on to become the recording venue for the *Plastic Ono Band* and *Imagine* albums.

It is believed Yoko Ono, George Harrison, and Ringo Starr, who sold the mic, also used it during recording sessions. Mick Cronin said he and his brother Johnny, who have been fans of the Beatles for as long as he can remember, could not believe their luck when their bid was accepted for what is a stunning piece of Beatles music history.

'It's like the Holy Grail to us; we can't believe we actually have it,' said Mick. 'We had it sent away to Germany to have it checked out and make sure it still works because it hasn't been switched on since 1971. We didn't want to damage it; we're looking forward to the day we can sing into it,' he continued.

'It's cool that we have a little piece of history. I mean Phil Spector would have had his hands on it – I know he was a nutter and everything but he did record an awful lot of great songs,' Mick laughs. 'We certainly didn't expect that we'd actually get to purchase it. We were sure Liam Gallagher or someone would have come in with a huge bid. I mean, where was he that day?!' he jokes.

MOTORBIKE BURIED IN BOG RETURNS TO SHOP AFTER 50 YEARS

A MOTORBIKE THAT had been buried in a bog for over 20 years made a miraculous return to the Edenderry shop where it was bought 50 years ago.

The story of the NSU Quickly bike is the talk of both Edenderry and Carbury this week. It was sold to the late Tom Cox in Carbury by Liam Moran in Edenderry, and exactly 50 years to the day, the restored bike was returned to Liam for a ceremonial spin.

Liam had last rode the distinctive looking bike when he delivered it to the Coxes, and Tom Cox drove it for close to 25 years. His son Tom (Jr) tells the paper, 'It was used mainly for going around Carbury, Edenderry, Allenwood and Rathangan although he did use it occasionally for travelling up and down to Dublin while he was working on the building of Liberty Hall when his regular lift didn't work out, the round trip hard going when you consider that it had a top speed of approximately 25 miles per hour!'

The bike disappeared and Tom Jr and brother Jimmy found it buried in the family bog. They set about restoring it on a casual basis, and when they found the original delivery dockets, they sped up as they wanted to surprise the man who sold it to their dad on the 50th anniversary of the sale. When they got to Moran's shop, they reckoned that Tom had got a bargain in the £60 he paid for it. Liam Moran told the pair, 'It should have been more and it's not too late to settle up!'

HONEST DIRECTIONS

The *Connaught Telegraph* spotted a great letter to the editor, from a lady in Hampshire, in a recent edition of the *Daily Telegraph*, and it is gleefully reprinted. Lyn Leventon wrote:

> Sir, on a recent trip to Co. Mayo, we became hopelessly lost. My husband stopped the car and inquired of a young local boy: 'Excuse me, how do you get to Ballina?'
>
> He replied: 'My cousin takes me.'

It strikes me as an honest answer but perhaps not the one the English visitor was hoping for.

I've an idea, I'll give away my 100-foot ivy plant for charity

A MAN WHO DESCRIBED himself as 'an amateur gardener' managed to grow 100 feet of ivy inside his sitting room for the last ten years. Tim Manning told the *Corkman* that he bought the indoor ivy plant a decade ago and only needed to water it once a week and give it fertiliser once a year. He said the plant began to thrive, so much so that it began to grow up along the walls and across his ceiling.

But after 10 years of looking at the ivy, he has had enough of it and wants to give it away to anyone who wants it. 'Or I would like to give it to a charity; it was all getting a bit too much, really. It was taking over the room totally,' said Mr Manning, who lives in Mallow.

When asked if the ivy; which was by now also going across his window sill and covering the walls, ever got on his nerves, he said it did not. 'It just got too big. I measured it and it's 100 feet long. It was time for it to go really.' He said even he was 'amazed' at how much the ivy thrived and he described it as a plant that was able to survive very well on its own. He said with a smile that he is now looking forward to claiming back his sitting room.

HOLY COW! COW GIVES BIRTH TO QUADRUPLETS!

NORTH WEXFORD FARMER Nigel Bailey couldn't believe what he was seeing when a cow at his farm delivered not just one, not two, not even three, but an incredible four healthy calves. Quadruplet calves are rare, and even more remarkable is the fact that this productive bovine has produced a total of six calves in less than a year.

'She is a twin herself, and she had twins last year as a heifer,' Nigel told Fintan Lambe. 'This is her second calving. I knew she was in calf, and she wasn't in as good condition as I'd expect, so I thought it might be twins.' He checked the calving camera at 6.45 a.m. on the big day, and saw she had delivered the first calf. He went out to the shed, and the second calf came out, with just a little help from Nigel. 'The third one came out backwards, so I helped with that,' he said. 'With the fourth one, I had to get that out myself.

'I couldn't believe it when the feet appeared of the third one,' he said. 'I was going to check her anyway, and I checked to see there wasn't a fifth. That would have been a bit greedy, but there was no point in leaving it in there if it was there!'

The calves are doing well. They were kept under an infrared light for a few days, and are feeding three times a day. Nigel has only heard of four calves being born like this once before – and coincidentally, it happened to a friend of his in Limerick who had four Angus calves. 'He was in agricultural college with me,' he said. 'You wouldn't hear of it happening too often though. You'd mainly hear of twins.'

The four celebrity calves have proven a hit with the younger members of the Bailey family who are busy helping their dad with the new arrivals.

ALIEN WASHED UP ON KERRY BEACH

PHRONIMAS, DEEP-SEA creatures that inspired the *Alien* movies because of their practice of burrowing into their victims, were discovered on Ventry Beach last week. These tiny, see-through, parasitic creatures are normally found in deep oceanic waters and their discovery by a local marine biologist, Kevin Flannery, has baffled experts. Indeed, the discovery is believed to be the first time creatures of this kind have been found in Ireland.

They served as the inspiration for the beasts immortalised in the works of artist H. R. Giger and seen on the big screen in Ridley Scott's *Alien* and James Cameron's *Aliens*. Indeed, this real-life mini-monster and the Alien Queen do share some similarities according to Katie O'Dwyer from Dingle Oceanworld. 'Some of our information also indicates that it is actually the female Phronimas that burrow out these barrels as it provides protection for the eggs they lay,' she said. 'Phronimas normally live in deep, deep waters; the fact that they have washed up on the beach like this in west Kerry is very strange indeed – you could say they are "alien" to these waters,' she added.

Stop the lights and get stoned

SMOKING SPLIFFS AND cruising the cosmos is not what the many visitors to the heritage haven of Westport expect during their winter breaks. But, hey, man, you would forgive those dudes who hit town early last week for thinking they had inadvertently landed in the hometown of some famous South American drug lord.

Not only were the traffic lights decorated with symbols of the marijuana leaf but also rather strange graffiti – believed to symbolise the leaf – was spotted by our undercover photographer, who naturally assured us he has never inhaled any illegal substance, even while in the pursuit of breaking news stories.

Local sleuth Inspector Joe McKenna also confirmed to the *Mayo News* that he was aware of the symbols on the traffic lights. 'I saw the traffic lights and the symbols have since been removed. I believe that heart signs appeared around the same time on traffic lights in Galway city. The only concern we had was that they might distract motorists.'

He assured the *Mayo News* that Gardaí were not worried that the signs or the graffiti were the work of serious drug pushers. 'I believe this was simply a prank and there is no need for anyone to be concerned.' Phew! But what a buzz.

Corkman succeeds in having bail varied to attend hurling final

A CORKMAN charged with IRA membership and firearms offences has had his bail conditions varied so he can attend the All-Ireland Hurling Final.

The Corkman and another man were arrested in February in Togher by local detectives as part of an investigation into the activities of dissident republicans.

They were charged before the Special Criminal Court with IRA membership and with the unlawful possession of a semi-automatic pistol, a revolver and ammunition.

The Court fixed bail of an independent surety of €20,000 each and their own bond of €100. Other conditions included signing on daily at a garda station, surrendering their passports, obeying a curfew and not associating with anyone charged or convicted at the Special Criminal Court.

Mr Carroll returned to Court yesterday to apply to vary his bail conditions. Niamh Ó Donnabháin said he wished to go to the All-Ireland Hurling Final in Dublin on Sunday and was requesting that his curfew be lifted on Saturday and Sunday nights. The State consented and the variation was allowed.

HOLD YOUR HORSES – HOW SMALL IS ZORRO?

YAY OR NEIGH, Garryhill may be able to lay claim to a new title: home to Ireland's smallest pony. Zorro the miniature pony was meant to be small but not this small. He was born on Saturday morning coming in at 20 inches high and his young breeder, eleven-year-old Ross Foley, couldn't believe his eyes. 'He is like a Jack Russell, it's so funny,' said Ross's father Patrick who owns the High Nellies pub in Garryhill.

The Falabella pony is a rare miniature breed but is almost half the size of another pony, also a Falabella, born at the same address six weeks ago. Zorro is all black and very fast. His mother, Ginger, however, won't let onlookers get too close as she is very protective of her tiny bundle. 'He is smaller than a dog; he is just tiny,' laughed Patrick.

PET LAMB EXPOSES SHEEP RUSTLER

When a pet lamb ran to its owner at Milltown Mart, in County Kerry, the farmer caught sight of the rest of his flock of sheep that had been stolen the day before. However, the lamb's innocent approach exposed the guilt of a Ballyvourney sheep rustler. The lamb's owner, Pat Scannell, had gone to the mart to see if an attempt was being made to sell his stolen sheep. The animals were brought back to Clonkeen, where each lamb went immediately to its mother. A man later pleaded guilty to the theft of 17 sheep and was convicted before Kenmare District Court.

ELVIS TURNS UP IN ILLEGAL IRISH DUMP

Elvis had definitely left the building this week when a Wicklow County Council litter warden uncovered a dump site containing a quantity of Elvis memorabilia. An inspection carried out at Lamberton – an area that has been targeted regularly in recent months by illegal dumpers – revealed an array of collectable items, perhaps discarded by a disgruntled fan.

While evidence of ownership was not present, the goods were thought to have formed part of a collection and included replicas from the Graceland Archives, including a copy of a receipt for the purchase of a French poodle for $250 in 1958 in Memphis.

SEAMUS'S WORK-MANSHIP STILL APPRECIATED 50 YEARS LATER

THE OLD SAYING goes that 'they don't make them like they used to' and a story in the *Leitrim Observer* would seem to back up that theory! Workmen carrying out maintenance work at a convent in Dingle, County Kerry, got a pleasant surprise when they discovered an inscription on the roof in Coláiste Íde. The inscription read: 'S. Weldon, Electrician, Drumshanbo, Co Leitrim, 1961. It was a good job, good luck next man'.

Fifty years later the message was uncovered and the workmen asked Eddie Carr, from Calry, County Sligo, who was also working in the area at the time if he knew anybody by that name. Neither Eddie nor the telephone directory was able to shed any light on who S. Weldon may be, so contact was made with the *Observer*.

After further discussions, contact was made with Nancy Woods from Drumshanbo and she confirmed that a brother of hers, Seamus, did indeed work in Dingle at that time. Now living in Williamstown, Kells, County Meath, Seamus got a surprise to say the least when he received word of the inscription he made 50 years ago. 'I don't remember writing it but I probably wrote it in a few places,' noted Seamus, who had no difficulty recalling the time he spent in Dingle and the job carried out there.

When details of the note he wrote were relayed to him, Seamus joked, 'It must have been written in an idle moment!' Laughing about the unlikely re-encounter with something he did 50 years ago, he added, 'I thought it was only from the modern days you could be traced!'

School clean-up reveals eighteenth-century sword – hidden in teacher's drawer!

MYSTERY SURROUNDS THE discovery of an eighteenth-century sword in a north Galway secondary school – and now an appeal has been made for information about the weapon. The unusual discovery was made while clearing out a room in the old Coláiste Sheosaimh school in Glenamaddy. Nobody seems to know where it originated.

It was found in a drawer in the old vice-principal's office and could have been there for several decades. Information is now being sought about where the sword came from and who might have given it to the school all those years ago.

The sword is in a poor state of repair and was presented to the National History Museum, which believes that it dates back to the late 1700s. The Museum has now asked Glenamaddy Community School to try and find out more information about it.

JUDGE HAD WALLET RETURNED ... BY MAN UP IN COURT

A JUDGE WHO dropped his wallet on his way into Sligo Courthouse had it returned to him by a man who later appeared before him. As Judge Tony Hunt emerged from his car outside the building on Thursday he unknowingly let his wallet fall to the ground. It was subsequently picked up by a man from Tubbercurry; he handed it over to barrister Dara Foynes, who gave it to the Judge's tipstaff, who returned it.

When the Judge emerged onto the bench, he mentioned the fact he had dropped 'a personal item' on the way in. He said he had heard it had been handed in by a man from Tubbercurry and wondered if it was the same man who was due to appear before him.

Ms Foynes later confirmed to Judge Hunt that the defendant had handed in his wallet and that he was due for sentencing. The Judge asked if the defence or prosecution had any objection to his hearing the case and he was informed there wasn't. Judge Hunt said the good deed wouldn't have a bearing on the outcome.

MYSTERY LOTTO WINNER 'BRENDAN' IS FOUND!

FORGET ABOUT THE All-Ireland Semi-Final, the big news in Donegal this week was the search for a mystery winner of a Donegal GAA lottery who left just his first name and a wrong phone number on his ticket. For the past number of days, members of Letterkenny Gaels GAA Club have searched high and low for the winner of the €6,250 prize. All they knew was that his name was Brendan.

They tried to contact him but the phone number wouldn't connect. So the club put out an SOS, which ran in all the Donegal papers, asking for anyone called Brendan who might have bought a club lottery ticket to get in touch. They even put posters in dozens of bars with pictures of the winning ticket on it, hoping the winner would come forward after he identified his own handwriting.

And at the weekend, the 'real' Brendan – Brendan Duffy of Dromore in Letterkenny – was finally tracked down. He didn't even know about the fuss the club made looking for a lost lotto winner! According to club spokesman John McDermott, they received up to 50 responses – with some as far away as Australia and London.

'I was getting calls from all over the world – literally. I got calls from across Donegal and Ireland but also as far away as London and even Australia. We were able to rule them all out straight away because we knew we had a mobile phone number which was probably just slightly wrong.

'So when the real Brendan did call and he was just one number out – a three instead of a two – we knew we finally had our man,' said John. As it turned out, the 'real' Brendan was relaxing on Lough Keel in Donegal fishing when the story broke. He will be presented with his cheque next week and has promised a drink for his friends in McGinley's Bar.

COUNCIL BANS DIVING FOR RARE GOLF BALLS

DONEGAL COUNTY COUNCIL has been left in the 'rough' after divers began searching for priceless golf balls in Lough Salt. Divers have been searching for rare golf balls which were left behind by former Open Championship winner Tom Morris in the 1800s. The golfing legend is believed to have struck 20 of the gutta-percha golf balls, which are worth €20,000 each, into Lough Salt.

However, Donegal County Council is worried about an influx of divers, because the lough is the main public water supply for thousands of households. The Council said it is very concerned the water supply could be threatened by amateur divers searching for the golf balls.

'Lough Salt is one of the main sources of drinking water for Letterkenny and its environs,' the Council said yesterday in a statement. 'Any activity that could lead to a threat to the quality of this water is taken very seriously by the Council.'

It has been reported that golfing legend Tom Morris drove 20 gutta-percha golf balls into Lough Salt while he was designing the nearby Rosapenna golf course in 1891. The story of recent attempts to retrieve the balls from the lake has received widespread media attention nationally and internationally. Donegal County Council now fears the publicity will lead to more people diving for the balls.

'The Council wishes to advise that as a drinking water source, Lough Salt is a protected water body under the Water Framework Directive and the Council will take all measures necessary, within its powers, to prevent further use of this lake for such recreational use,' the statement continued.

'It should also be noted that Lough Salt is a deep lake and diving in the lake requires the use of specialist diving equipment operated by divers trained and capable of using such equipment.

'The only situation that the Council will consider in terms of granting permission to dive in Lough Salt will be in relation to emergency contingency planning in order to develop a planned response to an accident which results in a recovery operation from the waters of the lake.'

German football legend drops by Louth GAA club for pep talk

WHEN GLENMUIR FC'S DARRYL O'KANE took to Facebook asking if anybody fancied a game of football, he probably didn't expect to end up playing against a Champions' League and World Cup finalist that evening. But that's exactly what happened on Thursday evening when former Arsenal and Germany goalkeeper Jens Lehmann put on his football boots and played for an hour with shocked locals at Glenmuir's football pitch.

Darryl's father Tony said the unexpected visit came about thanks to former Glenmuir player Alan Clarke, who currently works with StatSports, which are used by the German national team. 'So he was up at the Aviva last week as Germany trained for their match with Ireland and he got talking to Jens and asked him would he like to come down to Dundalk for a couple of hours.

'Alan brought him up to our club here in Glenmuir and he chatted with us for a while before putting on his boots and playing with the lads for near an hour. The boys were a bit stunned to see Jens coming out but they were thrilled to play with such a big star of the game,' explained Tony.

Lehmann also found time to call around to Clan na Gael football club on Thursday evening, visiting the team as they prepared for their Intermediate Club Final against O'Connell's. As Maurice Harrisson, PRO for the Clans, explains, the visit wasn't planned and again came about through Alan Clarke.

'Alan is a former Clans player and he convinced Jens to call around to the boys on Thursday evening to give them a few words of advice for Sunday's final. He spoke to the lads for about fifteen minutes telling them to keep focused and how to cope with the pressure of big games. He had a pint of Guinness with us and signed autographs and posed for photos and all that. It was a bit surreal but it was great to meet him and we'd all like to thank Alan for making it happen,' added Maurice.

They shoot refs in Cavan

CAVAN GAA COUNTY BOARD are to enlist the help of local Gardaí in their investigations as to how a match official was struck in the foot by a discharge from a firearm on Sunday. The alleged incident took place at the 3G pitch at the rear of Kingspan/Breffni Park during the 2011 MHC final between Ballymachugh and Mullahoran.

Referee James Clarke (Killinkere) was in the middle of the pitch, but it was his cousin Barry, one of his umpires, who became the unlikely centre of attention when he heard shots ring out from behind the scoreboard-end of the pitch.

'I was standing at one post and my cousin Pat was at the other post when we heard a shot ring out in the second half,' he tells the paper. 'We could see a man about 100 yards away from us with a gun and a little brown and white dog. He looked like he was shooting for pheasants.

'Then, about ten minutes after the first shot, there was another bang and the small gate behind us rattled. I could feel something wheezing past the bottom of my trousers and the next thing was I found this impact on my foot. I could see pellets like big grains of sand just a few feet away from me ... luckily I was wearing big, strong boots.' The shocked 26-year-old was unhurt and continued to observe the play.

Cavan GAA secretary Liam McCabe who was at the match confirmed he heard a loud firecracker-like noise. The matter will be discussed at a County Board meeting and Gardaí have been alerted.

In an otherwise uneventful afternoon, two late goals helped Ballymachugh triumph by 3-8 to 3-6 in what was a thrilling final played in an excellent sporting manner.

POSTMAN'S SPEED FINE GOT LOST ... IN THE POST

The *Corkman* reports that postman Martin Busteed, of Mayfield, County Cork, was recently up in Macroom District Court for failure to pay a speeding fine. His defence? He claimed that he had never received the fine because it got lost in the post! The courtroom erupted in laughter at his excuse.

'You can see why we're all laughing,' Judge James McNulty remarked. 'We were all subconsciously thinking that the postal service has gone to hell.'

'I've seen it all,' Mr Busteed replied.

Judge McNulty accepted the defendant's explanation and struck out the case. If Judge James McNulty were to have stuck strictly to the 'letter' of the law, he would have punished Martin, so it was a surprise delivery for Busteed to have his excuse accepted. We think his decision 'properly addressed' the situation.

Goats swim to safety – no kidding

CAN GOATS SWIM? It was a question a lot of onlookers were pondering at the N5 at Chancery near Ballyvary on Thursday. Two goats – one billy, one nanny – were stranded in an adjoining field by rising flood waters, which threatened to drown them.

The goats, believed to be wild, were spotted marooned in the flooded field on Monday. They were on dry land but surrounded by water, as the nearby river had burst its banks. As the weather got wetter, so did the goats, and by Thursday afternoon, the water had crept up as high as their backs and they were over 100 metres from dry land.

Passer-by Olivia Mannion rang the Gardaí, who in turn contacted Mayo County Council's Veterinary Department, which referred the case to Civil Defence. There, Rose Doherty and Tom Walsh answered the unusual call. However, they could not launch their boat at the field in question, so Inland Waterways came to the rescue with a boat fitter for the purpose of rescuing two goats.

Perhaps reacting to so much supervision and intervention from a nanny state, the two goats gruffly refused to get into the boat when it landed beside them. They swam further into the depths of the flood, but the vigilant boat crew managed to turn them in the direction of dry land. With no little agility, the pair swam through the flood and eventually to safety. The question now is 'Could the goats not have swum to safety earlier and avoided the furore?' Perhaps, but maybe they wanted to milk their moment in the public limelight.

HEALY-RAES HATE JAZZ

At Kerry County Council's monthly meeting, Independent Councillor Danny Healy-Rae brought a motion before the council bemoaning the council's new phone system. The Killgarvin Councillor said that since the system was installed he had found it almost impossible to get through to certain departments and had been driven to distraction by annoying hold music.

In his motion Councillor Healy-Rae called on the Council to go back to the old system as 'it is not fair that the members of the public have to give the day listening to recorded messages and unsavoury music'. The 'unsavoury' music referred to by Councillor Healy-Rae was a piece of jazz that played while callers were on hold. It has since been replaced by a classical piece commissioned by Kerry County Museum several years ago.

Councillor Healy-Rae said the new system had caused him, his brother Independent TD Michael, and his son and fellow councillor Johnny serious disruption. 'It's a battle to get through to the switch. I've been wasting energy listening to a type of music I've never encountered. There's a time and a place for music and it's not in the morning when you're trying to help someone with a serious problem,' he said. 'Some mornings I've only succeeded with two phone calls before 10 a.m. I've been sitting there sweating, listening to music and nothing happening,' said Councillor Healy-Rae.

Responding to Councillor Healy-Rae's complaint council management said the delays he was encountering were most likely due to the huge volume of calls that come into county buildings on a daily basis. The new phone system was described as a very efficient system that would save the council up to €60,000 a year in call costs. Management did accept that the original choice of hold music wasn't the best. Director of Corporate Services John Flynn said that the jazz music had indeed 'driven everyone mad'.

ARAN ISLAND'S FIRST-EVER PARKING TICKET!

One Inis Mór driver made history in a way they'd rather forget when they became the recipient of the first-ever road traffic violation ticket issued on the Aran Islands. Community Warden Martin Mannion attached the dreaded paperwork to the window of a car at Kilronan Harbour on Monday morning as the new County Council Traffic Plan kicked in on Inis Mór.

The Plan was agreed by Galway County Council in 2011 and it came into effect on 1 January. It regulates parking and traffic movement in the vicinity of the newly developed harbour at Kilronan. The regulations also apply to an area in the Cill Éanna harbour part of the island.

MICE DRIVING STRADBALLY RESIDENTS UP THE WALLS FOR MONTHS

MICE ARE TRIGGERING the alarm at the newly renovated Arthouse studio and library. Since officially opening in mid-May, residents in the quiet area of the town claim that their sleep has been disturbed on an on-going basis by the 'alarm going off nearly once a week'.

One man who contacted the *Laois Nationalist* said, 'It was terrible here last Sunday morning. I was awakened by the alarm going off at about 6 a.m. But that's not been the first time it's happened. Since it was opened, I'd say it's been happening on a weekly basis. I've been to the library to complain about it on a few occasions and asked them why they can't just send someone in to shut off the alarm when it goes off. They told me they can't turn it off. I know that, on a least four occasions, they've had people in to try and fix it, but it's not working. No-one seems to know how to fix the problem.

'The ringing it makes, sure you might as well have it in your room for the noise it makes. I was told they don't know what triggers it. They said it has sensors built into the wall and can detect vibrations. We're of the opinion that it's mice running around in there that's setting it off.

'To think they paid over €1 million in doing up the old courthouse and couldn't get a small alarm system to work right, it's just a joke. It's driving us up the walls. We can't get a wink of sleep. Something will have to be done about it. It's not fair on the people who live here.'

NORTHSIDE PEOPLE

BAGS BONO TO ASK

THE QUESTION ALL

DUBLINERS WANT

TO KNOW

THE *NORTHSIDE PEOPLE* proves that regional, local newspapers are the ones who get the real news. They lead and the nationals follow. The local newspaper got what newspapers have been trying to get for ages, an interview with Bono, who was on hand for the launch of a book called *Finglas: A People's Portrait*. It's safe to say he's Finglas's most famous former resident, yet Ballymun also claims him as one of their own. So where exactly is Bono from?

Under the headline 'The world's most famous Northsider', Bono had this to say to try and settle the argument as to where he is actually from: 'Oh, that's a very, very deeply upsetting and divisive question. There was a load of rows on Cedarwood Road about that very fact, because when we moved to Cedarwood Road everyone was saying we lived in Ballymun.

'Then at some point, I think when the seven towers were built and had built a reputation, some of the snobs around wanted to say, "No, no, no we're from Finglas." So I asked my dad, who worked in the postal service, and he said, believe it or not, "One part of the road is Ballymun and one part of the road is Finglas," so you can say what you like.'

DECIES UNDER THREAT FROM FAIRY WRATH

FORGET ABOUT THE general election, don't fret about the IMF and let the international bondholders go to blazes: we are in deep trouble because some very stupid vandals have cut down the famous Fairy Tree on the Comeragh Mountain Drive.

The foul deed was done under the cover of darkness but, of course, those that committed the desecration will find no hiding place on this earth. They might evade the Gardaí but the Curse of the Sidhe (fairies) will follow them until they make amends and beg for mercy.

The fear of local people in the Comeraghs is that the Sidhe will also take revenge on the overall county where the atrocity occurred. If they are not placated, the fairies may cast a spell of doom over us all. The Decies will never win an All-Ireland or a Cup Final, we'll never have a government minister or a university and, worst of all, the Sidhe may silence all our music

and song, and for good measure, poison all the drinking water in the land. These are serious dudes best left alone and they are never, ever to be messed around. A pox on those who upset their Lordships on Earth.

The Fairy Tree, a Munster landmark, was visited by thousands of people every year, with many hanging ribbons. It stood on a stretch of the 'magic road' where cars appeared to travel backwards uphill, and where the road was full of ghosts, including highwayman Crotty the Robber, who was meant to watch over the Comeraghs. Where the feck was he when the vandals struck?

Now, to placate the fairies, it is said the only thing to do is to plant a cluster of hawthorn, oak and ash on the spot as a peace offering. Such a gesture of good will and respect might just be the thing to sooth the rage of the Sidhe and negate their revenge.

A dung deal at Ardfert art exhibition

The normal place one would expect to see cow dung is on a farm, but this is not the case in the Old Forge, Ardfert, as a painting made from the animal waste is currently hanging on the wall at an art exhibition housed there. The painting, by local artist Angie Plastow, is one of many varieties of art being displayed by six Kerry artists and one artist from Dublin.

Angie Plastow, originally from Kent in England, has Irish parents, Maurice Dore from Lixnaw and Rita Costello from Abbeydorney, and decided to move to Ireland five years ago. Angie was in a relationship with a farmer for a few years and through this she began to milk the cows on the farm. 'I got my inspiration for my painting, *Effluence*, from looking at the changing patterns in cow dung over the various seasons,' explains Angie.

'Cow dung is considered by most people as distasteful, dirty and pungent, but it isn't – it is organic and part of the cows' cycle which is natural. Cows are seen as dumb animals but their dairy products feed us which is very important.'

'The painting does not smell as I used coffee grounds and mandarin oil to combat the odour,' said Angie. So far Angie has had one interested buyer for the piece which costs €500.

'A lady was inquiring about purchasing the painting but her husband was not too keen and said "You must be joking me if you think I'm paying €500 to hang a pile of cow shit on my wall",' laughed Angie.

Bronze Age body discovered in 'lean to'

A BODY DATING back to the early Bronze Age has been discovered by a man who was building a 'lean to' in his back garden in Collinstown, just outside Mullingar. Local man Pat Tiernan unearthed the body, crouched beside a food vessel, after he unearthed some ground just outside his back kitchen window where he was building a fabled Irish 'lean to' shed.

Pat, who has lived in his home with wife Cathy and son Turlough for the past five years, couldn't quite believe his eyes. 'It's crazy to think he's been lying there for over three thousand years,' he said. 'I stood in the kitchen window last Sunday after a feed of drink Saturday night, doing a bit of washing up, and I looked out the kitchen window and I thought – that looks like a bone hanging out of the bank!

'I went out and had a look and that's when I copped the pot. It looked like an imprint in the soil, so I dusted it off and a piece just fell off. I thought that's a bit older than your normal earthenware!'

The 3,000-year-old remains, which have not yet been identified as either male or female, were found in a crouched position beside a food vessel – and have been deemed by the National Museum to be part of an 'important' Early Bronze Age burial practice. They say the person was of some importance in the community as he was buried with the large bowl.

RELIEF AS KENNY JUMPER RETURNED

There was a close call for Dundalk FC Manager Stephen Kenny, who nearly lost a jumper in a local cafe. Much like any normal day, Mr Kenny was enjoying a coffee and a read of the newspaper at Panama Cafe on Market Square. Kenny, who is a sometime patron of the popular cafe, eventually finished his break, got up and paid before leaving the establishment.

However, it soon became clear that one of his favourite jumpers that he had with him when he entered the cafe was no longer in his possession. Kenny, who is enjoying his tenure as Dundalk Manager in one of its most successful campaigns in years, immediately began a search.

Speaking to the *Dundalk Democrat*, owner of Panama Stephen Egan said he initially suspected St Patrick's or Drogheda United fans had something to do with it. 'Stephen came back and we presented him with the jersey. In fact he had just left it behind on the seat. He was delighted to have it back. No Drogheda or Pats fans were involved in its abduction!' Let's hope the safe return of the jumper heralds more good luck for the rest of the season.

Priests and piracy: retailers reel from illegal downloading

JUST HOW ACCEPTABLE illegal downloading of copyrighted material has become is illustrated by the community of Limerick priests who are watching movies at their film club weeks before they are shown in the cinema. Paul Flynn who has been in the DVD rental business, at Moviedrome on Henry Street, for 17 years said one of his favourite customers was a Limerick cleric and film buff, who had broken the first rule of film club by talking about film club.

'He's been coming in to me for the last five or six years. A lovely man who loves his old films. Back in January, he mentioned he had watched *Lincoln* the night before. Maybe I'm naive and I asked had they shown it early in the cinema or something and he said, "No, we have a film club once a week and we watched it up at the monastery." I said that's only opening in the cinema today. He said, "Well, we watched *Django Unchained* last week, which I found very violent; we watched *Les Misérables* the week before and *Zero Dark Thirty* the week before that." I said to him none of those films had actually opened apart from *Les Mis*,' said Mr Flynn.

That a community of priests might not consider piracy has anything to do with the seventh commandment – the one about stealing – shows just how ingrained illegal downloading has become.

'They don't see it as stealing. Three years ago I did say to the *Limerick Leader* that we were not going to have a record store in Limerick. I didn't think it was going to be as fast as it was but it has come to pass.

'You can't really blame Joe Soap for downloading. It's the guys uploading who are my bugbear. And then there's the Googles of this world who really don't have a conscience. They were able to turn off child pornography overnight, a click of a switch and it was pretty much gone. They can do the same with torrents and file-sharing websites very easily but they are making an absolute fortune from advertising revenue. You had Rupert Murdoch, and I know he's not a paragon of virtue, criticising their business model as not quite theft but abetting,' said Mr Flynn.

When Mr Flynn made his prediction about the end of music retailing in the city centre three years ago this week, Empire Music had just stopped selling CDs from the major labels, with piracy as a major factor.

But Moviedrome – which is an internet cafe and offers game rental and PC repair as well as the latest DVD releases – is about to resuscitate the music store in the city centre. The business already offers a service whereby customers can order records, and stocks independent Irish music releases. And deals with the record labels will see major music releases appear on the shelves in the coming weeks.

'I know it's only a niche and I'm hitching my rope to a falling star because music, unfortunately, is going only one direction. But I'm trying to fill the gap that HMV have left. If it fails I have enough going on here and it won't put me out of business.

'I'm doing DVDs for 20 years and I'm still making mistakes in ordering so if I start ordering in music without doing my homework, I might not be at it very long. I'd order with my heart rather than my head and order 30 copies of the new Bowie album and one Lady Gaga and I could end up with 29 Bowie left and no Gaga but we'll have to see how it goes.'

Whether it's an illegal download site or a legitimate on-line operation, Mr Flynn believes street retailers can go the extra mile for customers in a way Amazon never can. 'Just go into O'Mahony's and see the service you get. Nobody can tell you Amazon can offer that experience. When you walk into O'Mahony's you have a great range, you have excellent staff and you are in an environment that wows you aesthetically and architecturally. And I'd like to think that Moviedrome can offer you a similar experience of the kind you won't get whether you are on Netflix or downloading.'

Longford snubbed by Google Maps

There is widespread outrage brewing over Longford's scandalous absence from the map of Ireland on Google Maps. The town is peculiarly referred to as 'Prospect Wood'. One can zoom in to see various towns such as Edgeworthstown, Lanesborough and Ballymahon highlighted. Moving northwards, one can even see small towns in Cavan such as Village and Killeshandra also flagged (obviously the whizzes who run Google Maps are major fans of the Wolfe Tones).

Quite how the employees of Google Maps got the impression this town went by the name of a decade-old estate on the edge of the town is unknown at this stage.

Longfordians are used to complaining of being ignored and overlooked by the media but this snub really is the most galling yet. Despite the sterling efforts this summer of Paul Barden, Sean McCormack, Keith Gillespie and Tony Cousins to put Longford on the map, Google Maps are having none of it.

Google Maps mysterious bias against midland towns with League of Ireland soccer teams is also in evidence in the fact that Athlone is also absent from the map, replaced by Clonbrusk. This offers some solace for Longford people in that we're not alone in this fight. However, the time has come to end all this; let's resolve to put Longford on the map.

Piddle-riddle as 62 bottles of urine found in Glanmire

Residents of Glanmire have been perplexed by a piddle-riddle, after 62 bottles of urine were found dumped in a ditch. The urine-filled plastic Coca-Cola bottles were dumped in Glyntown, a scenic area plagued by illegal dumping, and were found by a woman walking in the area on Saturday.

This waste deposit of filled and half-filled 500 ml bottles in plastic bags has baffled locals, such as local councillor Labour's Noel Costello. He told the *Cork Independent* that locals have been unable to make sense of the peculiar discovery. 'If someone had been caught short, they would have gone in a ditch. This is very strange. Who fills bottles of urine and throws it out? Some of the bottles were only half full.'

He suggested that someone could be living without toilet facilities in the area and discarding bodily fluids in Glyntown. 'But again, that makes no sense,' said Councillor Costello. 'They would need a car to drive out and again, why go into bottles?'

A total of 45 bottles were discovered on Saturday, while another 17 bottles have been found close to the initial dumping area. 'From the smell of the liquid, it's pretty obvious what it is. Some is also older than others, judging by the smell and the overgrowth in the ditch. We believe the smaller amount of bottles has been there over six months. It makes no sense at all,' Councillor Costello said.

BENNY AND THE JETS

A CASTLEDERG AMATEUR radio enthusiast has become the unlikely hero of a double aeroplane rescue, all from the comfort of his own home. Benny Young (29) was turning the dial on his FT 2000 ham radio on the night of Monday 29 October, the same time that Hurricane Sandy began its lashing of the American eastern seaboard, when he heard '... mayday, mayday, mayday ...'

Immediately Benny started broadcasting on that frequency. Details are still emerging, but it turns out that a transatlantic flight from Dublin bound for Boston was 180 miles from destination when disaster struck. Because of the storm, Boston's Logan International Airport was having trouble with electricity supply and the Instrument Landing System – which guides pilots to and their planes – wasn't functioning properly. Subsequently, Air Traffic Control couldn't hear the mayday call and the pilot couldn't hear any broadcast from ground control. Enter the Derg man.

'I responded to the plane, gave my call sign, MI3 JQD, and asked them what was wrong,' Benny explained. 'It was the night that the hurricane was giving Boston the jolly, as they say, and the flight couldn't hear anything on the ground. They must have thought they were going to be able to and before the weather turned. Then the storm arrived and they didn't think they were going to reach Boston at all.'

According to Benny, during a crisis situation when phone networks are down and electricity supplies are unreliable, an emergency network of US amateur radio operators swings into action. Knowing this, the Derg man tuned into the American emergency frequency and was able to contact 'Bob', an amateur radio operator who in turn contacted Logan International.

By relaying messages from the flight to 'ob and then to Air Traffic Control – and vice versa – Benny was able to guide the plane to safety, re-routing to an airport in Buffalo where a miraculous landing occurred. Benny continued, 'There were times the airport could hear the plane and there were times they couldn't. I tried to help as much as I could, relaying messages from the plane to the ground and then from the ground to the plane. I kept writing it all down as well: heading, altitude, speed, wind speed – and then I passed this on.

'I logged everything in my logbook as I went along. It worked out all right in the end,' he added humbly.

Amazingly, lightning struck twice on the same night, and when it emerged that a second flight was in trouble, an American Airlines plane from Heathrow to Boston, Benny stepped up to the plate once again. 'I did the same thing and this time the plane was re-routed to JFK,' the local member of Strabane Amateur Radio Society remarked. 'It was one of those freak incidents ... Nothing like this has ever happened to me before.

'It was some rush too but I tried to keep calm and I kept writing the altitude and heading and all the rest down. I had just been turning the dial on the radio and this was what I landed in.'

A fork-lift driver for L. W. Surphlis & Son, Benny admits he potentially saved lives that day – and he said he'd do it again. 'I didn't mind doing it and if I heard it again I'd be back in, flat to the tin. It was some buzz.'

Commending Benny on his quick thinking and calm head, Terry Whyte from Strabane Amateur Radio Society said the Castlederg man should be proud of himself. 'Certain stations are set aside on these bands and Benny was at the right frequency at the right time,' the club secretary remarked. 'He recorded everything in his log but we still gave him a good grilling at the last club meeting – in fact everyone else is jealous. This kind of thing is an amateur radio man's dream.'

POTHOLES SO BAD ASTRONAUTS COULD TRAIN IN THEM

'ASTRONAUTS IN TRAINING could practise their moon walks along Green Lane,' joked Councillor Rody Kelly at Thursday's meeting of Carlow Town Council. The Green Lane was raised by Councillor John Cassin who said the surface of the road was 'a disaster' and wondered if any improvement works could be done.

Cassin was supported by Councillor Ann Ahern who said, 'I nearly had a mini-heart attack when I saw them digging up the entrance at Rathnapish the other day.' She added the road was 'like the bumpers'.

'If there were any astronauts in training they could practise there,' quipped Councillor Kelly. Town engineer Brian O'Donovan said the road will be completely resurfaced when the main drainage scheme is completed.

SLIGO MAN WON'T REBUILD HIS WALL

A SLIGO MAN is refusing to rebuild his wall because it keeps getting hit by cars. The sleepy Sligo hamlet of Ballyrush has been the scene of an exorbitant number of car accidents since last autumn, as motorists have failed to manoeuvre a turn and ended up knocking into a nearby wall. Martin's wall has seen its fair share of knocks – twenty smashes in under a year – and he is blaming who else but the local Council for the surge in crashes.

Thankfully, there have been no injuries, but Ballyrush man Martin O'Sullivan has said he'll not reinstate the stone wall for fear of further crashes causing injuries. 'The crashes have all been happening since last autumn. The Council resurfaced the road and whatever work they did has left the surface extremely slippery after rain, and cars just skid all over the place,' Martin said.

The bend is close to the River Unshin and the road had been suffering from severe flooding, which the Council managed to cease with their development. This work, though, has left the corner extremely hazardous to drivers and Martin says that even his neighbours have spun out a few times. Now the road is flooded with debris from plastic bumpers and fragments from broken lights accompanied by countless skid marks. One car even ended up in his garden lately and during the ice last winter five people hit the wall.

'I would say that twenty motorists have hit the wall in the past year. I've decided that there's no point in rebuilding it, as I'd be afraid making it stronger might cause a fatality.' Martin would like the Council to do something about the road surface to avoid any more accidents.

Shovel for your supper!

A MACROOM COUNCILLOR has warned he will soon lose weight – because he will be banned from his favourite restaurant if the potholes outside the establishment are not fixed.

Councillor Martin Coughlan (Labour) told this week's meeting of Macroom Town Council that the proprietors of Granville's Bar and Restaurant deserved better pavements outside their premises having paid substantial development charges to the local authority.

'Every time I go in there the same topic comes up – the state of the footpath outside. I'll soon be losing weight because I won't be allowed in to eat,' Councillor Coughlan quipped.

The naked mass-goer

THE 8.30 A.M. MASS in Saint Peter's and Paul's Church in Port-laoise was delayed for a short while on Sunday morning to allow Gardaí time to remove a naked man from the church.

Churchgoers were left speechless when they entered the church to see the man, who is in his mid-50s and single, sitting alone without any clothes on.

The congregation left the naked man alone until two Gardaí arrived at the church and escorted the man, who was by now covered with a white robe-type garment, out into a waiting garda patrol car.

Graveyard gates locked after Del Boy's van makes appearance on tombstone

A DECISION HAS been made to lock the gates of a north Mayo cemetery after graves were damaged by large machinery which was erecting 'monsters of headstones'. Among the headstones were a marble version of Del Boy's three-wheeled van and a massive Romanesque depiction of the last supper.

Members of a newly formed committee at Lisheen Graveyard will be the key-holders at the cemetery and will have to be contacted by anyone proposing to undertake work inside the cemetery gates. The drastic action was taken after heavy machinery was driven over unmarked graves in recent weeks. Locals are calling for strict regulations to stamp out giant headstones that are out of place in their rural graveyard.

'It's so disrespectful. People come into the graveyard and knock walls to get their own headstones up. Everyone is so annoyed; they should have to get planning permission for the size of the headstones,' said one disgruntled local who has family buried in the cemetery.

Reporter Marian Harrisson estimates that over €50,000 has been spent on elaborate marble and granite sculptures that 'dominate the skyline in the cemetery'. The Del Boy Reliant Regal van is seen by many as being the tipping point.

Local Councillor Eddie Staunton tells the paper, 'The situation will be investigated and the graveyard will be put back to its former glory, and that has been promised.'

GUESS WHO'S IN THE COFFIN

A HALLOWEEN GAME, 'Guess who is in the coffin', attracted big crowds to the Red Deer pub in Pallasgreen. Four men wearing wellingtons carried the coffin into the pub and laid it gently on the pool table.

A GYPSY WOMAN PUT A SPELL ON ME

She wore green contact lenses with brown pupils. She had a stone in her upper right tooth and she managed to steal thousands of euros – all because she hypnotised her victim. This is not the plot of a 'CSI' drama; this happened last week in the centre of Carlow town, on Tullow Street to be precise.

Carlow Gardaí are currently in the midst of a puzzling investigation after a woman came into the station to report the creepiest of crimes. The 29-year-old, who lives in the town, reported being hypnotised and robbed of thousands after she was approached by a woman, described as being an 'Eastern European gypsy' possibly of 'Polish or Roma' origin.

The incident occurred at 3 p.m. on Tuesday, 23 August, when the victim was strolling down Carlow town's main shopping street. She claims to have been approached by the gypsy, whom she described as being aged around 23 to 25 and having long black hair.

She somehow managed to put the woman under a hypnotic spell and then led her to a bank where the victim emptied her account of thousands of euro. She also handed over her wedding ring and mobile phone to the mysterious stranger. Sergeant John Foley of Carlow Garda Station admitted this was the first crime of its kind reported at the station, but added that Gardaí were 'taking it at face value at the moment – we're treating it seriously'.

LIMERICK ACTOR SEEKS REFUND AFTER ANGLE GRINDER RUINS PLAY

LEADING LIMERICK ACTOR Liam O'Brien is seeking a refund from the Belltable Arts Centre after he bought a ticket to see a play that was spoiled by noise from machinery outside.

Members of the audience attending *Love, Peace and Robbery* at the newly renovated theatre were surprised to hear the loud sound of an angle grinder and a revving engine shortly after the actors took to the stage.

The noise was coming from a garage located in the laneway off Mallow Street behind the Belltable stage. Garage owner Mick Daly was accused of disrupting the gala opening of the theatre last November by operating his equipment at show time. 'I'm not doing anything that I haven't been doing over the past 40 years. It's not a funeral parlour I'm running,' he said.

Daly has been in dispute with the Belltable since renovations began at the theatre and has alleged that his business was adversely affected by the work. He claimed renovations failed to comply with conditions of planning attached by An Bord Pleanála. This was denied by the Belltable's management.

Mr O'Brien, who was in the audience to support friends during the opening night of the production by the Magic Roundabout Theatre Company, said his enjoyment of the show was spoiled by the sound of a car being revved up, banging metal and an angle grinder being used. He said the noise is even louder for the actors on stage who are trying to remember their lines and deliver a good performance, which he said they succeeded in doing despite the distraction.

It wasn't Mr O'Brien's first experience of the external noise at the Belltable. 'This matter has been ongoing since November 2010, and I have personally had seven shows ruined by this issue.'

The issue was most delightfully followed up in October of that year when legendary Irish rockers Granny's Intentions were preparing to play a couple of comeback shows, over 30 years since they split up.

HUGHIE'S REMARKABLE REUNION WITH OLD 'FRIEND'

SOON TO BE 90 years old, Hughie O'Donovan of Kilmore, Innishannon, had a remarkable reunion with an old friend recently. The event took place on a sunny Saturday evening on the grounds of the historic Innishannon House Hotel. Present with Hughie were members of his family; many old friends from the world of farming, hunting, sport in general; neighbours and his many colleagues from the music scene and from business.

The sounds of Liam Curtin's hunting horn heralded the arrival – just before the sun began to sink in the west – of the sound of an engine with smoke pluming into the evening air, led by two pipers from the Bandon and District Pipe Band, Finbarr and Jill Finn. There emerged a tractor driven by John Desmond.

And much to Hughie's surprise, this was the first tractor he owned – a 1953 Ferguson TEF 20 Diesel, which he bought from the late Pascal McSweeney of Bandon for £150 pounds in 1968. He kept this machine until 1974, and upon the advice of his late and beloved wife Mary, he sold it to the Barry Bros of Ballymurphy. It was then sold on to John Noel and Mark O'Sullivan of Killeady.

The dreaded return of the COMMITTEE

'TIS THE SEASON for spotting committees in Castlepollard; this rare and elusive creature seems to be driven into the open in search of new members as soon as the hour goes back and the long evenings draw in. Observers have noted a pattern to this animal's behaviour which links cold, dark winter nights with long journeys into sparsely populated areas, but as yet not enough data has been gathered to provide a single reasonable explanation for this activity.

Recent sightings of the animal in its juvenile stage, or 'forming', has been reported with a community committee for promotion of Castlepollard and a historical committee both observed in the town. There have also been sightings three weeks in a row of a committee in Coole objecting to proposed turbines in the area; observers call this the 'storming' stage and expect to see many sightings of this committee in full flight over the next few months.

Mature committees are also expected, although they don't have the energy and enthusiasm of juveniles, often spending many hours 'performing'. Ballycomoyle AGM, on 17 November, will offer many committee fans the opportunity to view a committee in its natural habitat.

Chamber of Horrors' bells ring in New Year

AS THE PEOPLE of Collooney stepped outside their front doors to ring out the old and ring in the new, they were pleasantly drawn together by the mellow sound of distant bells coming from the direction of Glebe House, which was compared to the 'tolling of the bell in Madame Tussaud's Chamber of Horrors'. Thanks to Pat Durcan of Glebe House, his wife Nichola (established classical musician) and their family for adding mystery and class to the occasion.

Puss Sunday – why single women wear their hair in a bun!

During 'saraft' (the period of time between Christmas and Lent), single women in the locality were known to wear their hair in a bun or 'coicín' to indicate they were available for courting. If the 'saraft' passed and a woman sporting a coicín was not courted, it was said that she'd be so unhappy on the first Sunday of Lent that she would have a 'puss', or sour expression. Therefore, the first Sunday of Lent was known as 'Puss Sunday'.

Eiffel Tower rebuilt in Dungarvan

THAT MAGNIFICENT REPLICA of the Eiffel Tower, the most historic landmark in Paris, which has been erected at the entrance to the shopping centre, has well and truly caught the imagination of the general public.

The forty-foot-high Eiffel Tower becomes an even more spectacular spectacle when darkness falls, as it is then lit up from head to toe and really is an eye-catching sight to behold.

We understand it has been erected by Tiffany's Restaurant as part of a build up to Valentine's Day, and all credit, and indeed congratulations, to the boss man Mustafa at Tiffany's on this blockbuster initiative.

GREETINGS FROM

Dungarvan

GRANNY'S INTENTIONS SEND MICK DALY ABROAD TO AVOID DISRUPTIONS DURING BELLTABLE GIGS

SEMINAL LIMERICK BAND Granny's Intentions, who have reformed for three sold-out gigs in the Belltable, have come up with a unique solution to ensure that theirs will be the only music coming out of the theatre this weekend. The band have made a present of a trip to Paris to garage owner Mick Daly, located in the laneway behind the Belltable, whose on-going row with the theatre has seen productions repeatedly disrupted since it was renovated over 12 months ago.

'We are sending Mike to Paris; we have to because he is in a "grinding mood" at the moment,' explained Cha Haran of the band, who is a school friend of Mr Daly. 'If we are to play and have three successful gigs we will have to have a bit of silence so our music will come out over Michael's. That is part of the deal.' Fellow Granny Jack Costelloe said, 'It is to give peace a chance!' The band has paid for Mr Daly to fly to Paris, covering all of his costs, flights and accommodation.

Noise emanating from Daly's laneway garage has repeatedly disrupted productions in the theatre since it was renovated last year, the sounds of angle grinders and revving engines having been heard during productions, as well as delaying proceedings when Arts Minister Jimmy Deenihan officially opened the building recently.

Mr Daly claimed he is simply 'going about his work'. 'I am working here every day for 40 years. I work at eight or nine o'clock; I am doing that for the last 40 years,' he said.

PONY GOES FOR A FIVER WHILE HEN FETCHES €15

A PONY WAS sold at Millstreet Fair for €5 while a feathery hen made €15 in what has left many Duhallow punters shaking their heads at an unusual economic trend. The fair attracted crowds to the town over the weekend. However, according to Councillor Noel Buckley, despite horses going up and down the town it was the hens on sale that drew the most looks and interest. 'It's the talk of the town that a pony was sold for €5 while a hen made €15. It's unbelievable stuff,' laughed Councillor Buckley.

Loughnavalley notes sweet-toothed litter-bugs

IT'S SO DISCONCERTING when (let's be kind here) a person or persons discard their rubbish in our lovely little village. It would appear that the tidier the area is, the more attractive it is to these neanderthals to rubbish. We can only hope that the Andrews Liver Salts are working well for the person(s) who consumed eleven (eleven!!) boxes of Roses over the festive season. You will be pleased to note that thanks to vigilance, we are fairly certain who this person (?) is. Details are with the County Council. Shame on you.

Acknowledgements

BRINGING THE LOCALS national is largely thanks to Hector Ó hEochagáin and Alan Swan, who took a chance on giving a few minutes of national radio to a lad they had literally met in a pub. Just prior to him securing a breakfast radio slot with RTÉ 2FM, Hector and I were at a Mark Lanegan gig, where I reeled off a variety of fairly big stories from the medium-sized towns of Ireland. When he got the breakfast gig, his producer Alan was next to be hit with a volley of stories. I was on air the following Tuesday – and 'Medium-Sized Town, Fairly Big Story' was born. Big thanks to them, to all at RTÉ Galway and to the soldiers of the dawn for three memorable years.

Huge thanks to all the team at 'Ireland AM' on TV3, both behind and in front of the camera. It really is a massive honour and a thrill to be able to tell a couple of hundred thousand viewers of this excellent show which Fairly Big Stories are making the headlines in the Medium-Sized Towns of Ireland.

It was with fortunate timing that I met Deirdre Nolan from Gill & Macmillan. She won't know this, but her belief in getting this book off the ground genuinely turned my life around at a very strange juncture – and not the one which normally results in the purchase of a motorbike and a leather jacket. Fair play to her and to all at Gill & Macmillan for taking the chance on a man who had a shed full of stories. I can't thank enough the wonderful Fuchsia MacAree for her vivid, warm and unique illustrations.

Nothing on this earth can compare to my wife, Deirdre, and children, James and Emily. I love you all, thanks for putting up with the papers and the madness. A special thanks to Ann and Kevin Duncan for putting a roof over our heads when we needed it. A big thanks as ever to my dad, Seamus, mum, Doreen, brother, Justin, and sister, Celina.

With so many stories covering all of Ireland and so many of its glorious regional papers to choose from – you want to see what we left out! – it would be impossible to name and thank every single journalist, correspondent and contributor. Hopefully I have acknowledged most of you in the Roll of Honour. Many stories were not by-lined, so if I have forgotten anyone please let me know and we'll get you next time.

And, finally, if you like this book or enjoy the radio and TV slots, please go out and buy your local newspaper! There are well over fifty in the country and they are the lifeblood of any local community. Too few of us know who our neighbours are; we don't know who our politicians are; we don't know what's on; and lots of us don't know a thing about where we live. But if you buy your local newspaper, you can change all that! Without our local newspapers, the Medium-Sized Towns of Ireland would be fairly dull places indeed.

Roll of Honour

There are many journalists whose stories helped in the creation of this book. Please take a bow:

Joe Barrett – *Laois Nationalist*

Joe Leogue – *The Corkman*

Cormac Campbell – *Newry Reporter*

Marisa Reidy, Dónal Nolan, Marian O'Flaherty, Lorraine Walsh, Brendan McCarthy, Kevin Hughes – *The Kerryman*

John O'Connor (a legend), Dermot Keyes – *Munster Express*

Niall O'Driscoll, Leo McMahon, Áilín Quinlan, Louise Rosengrove, Sean Mahon – *Southern Star*

Edwin McGreal, Áine Ryan, Ciara Galvin – *Mayo News*

Finian Coghlan – *Athlone Advertiser*

Mairead O'Shea, Ciara McCaughley – *Roscommon Herald*

Carol Byrne, John Galvin – *Clare Champion*

Donal O'Regan, Alan English, Gerard Fitzgibbon, Mike Dwane, Alan Owens, Áine Fitzgerald – *Limerick Leader*

Patrick Conboy, Rachel Masterson, Sheila Reilly – *Longford Leader*

Fintan Lambe, Maria Pepper, David Looby – *Wexford People*

Dick Hogan, Damien Maher, Paul O'Donovan, Seamus Kiernan, Larry Cooney, Michelle Crawley, James Wims – *Westmeath Topic*

Karen Downey, Kieran Galvin, Tadhg Carey – *Westmeath Independent*

Ian Cameron, Martin Grant – *Dundalk Democrat*

Natalie Burke – *Malahide Gazette*

Damian McCarney, Linda O'Reilly, Kevin Carney – *The Anglo-Celt*

Niamh O'Donoghue – *Leinster Leader*

Lynda Kiernan – *Leinster Express*

Mary Ellen Breen – *Waterford News and Star*

Hubert Murphy, Martin Pepper – *Drogheda Independent*

Michael Devlin – *Ulster Herald*

Colin Lacey – *Kerry's Eye*

William O'Connor – *Tallaght Echo* and *Echo Newspapers*

Colin McGann, Andrew Hamilton, Emmet Moloney – *Clare People*

Sam Matthews, Trevor Spillane, Brian Keyes – *Kilkenny People*

Seán Feeny – *Donegal News*

Hillary Martyn, Conor Harrington, Lorraine O'Hanlon – *Galway Independent*

Dave O'Connell, Enda Cunningham, Dara Bradley, Denise McNamara, Declan Tierney, Máirtín Ó Catháin – *Connaught Tribune*

Mairéad Wilmot, Clare Minnock, Conal O'Boyle, Suzanne Pender, Sarah Rowe – *Carlow Nationalist*

Chris Donegan – *Impartial Reporter*

Niamh Devereux, Anna Hayes, Saoirse McGarrigle, Dan Walsh – *Wexford Echo Group*

Maria Herlihy, Sheila Fitzgerald, Bill Browne, Brendan Malone – *The Corkman*

Michael Treacy, Chris Fingleton – *Laois Nationalist*

Laura Ryder – *Offaly Independent*

James Laffey – *Western People*

Neil Fetherston – *Northside People*

John FitzSimmons, Gerry Buckley, Una D'Arcy, Eilis Ryan – *Westmeath Examiner*

Noelle Finegan, Ken Davis, John Donoghue – *Meath Chronicle*

Eve Kelliher – *Killarney Advertiser*

Deirdre O'Shaughnessy – *Cork Independent*

Noel O'Driscoll – *Kildare Nationalist*

Paddy Walsh – *Donegal Democrat*

Jessica Quinn, John Kelly, John Galvin – *Clare Champion*

Colm Gannon – *Mayo Advertiser*

Aoife McKeever – *Newry Reporter*

Declan Howard, Ellen Lynch – *The Avondhu*

Mark Cagney, Anton Savage, Sinéad Desmond, Anna Daly, Jody Sheridan, Sally McLoughlin, Sinéad Ryan, Maeve Feehan, Sophie Kelly – 'Ireland AM', TV3

Amy Fitzgibbon, Roslyn Martyn, Doireann Wylde, Doyler et al – RTÉ Galway

Justin Casey, Tony Palmer - IT support

Colin Rhatigan, Marty Mulligan, Moff, Robert Duncan Removals

MICKEY MOUSE IS A CAT

Trespassers claimed to be jogging to lose weight

COUNCIL CANNOT THINK OF ANYTHING

M:
N

Fa
re
pl
af
gl

DOGS IN MOUNT-

MELLICK MAY

SOON BE IN

NAPPIES

Council paints yellow lines around parked car

'I DID COU

Hole for sale in Longford

KE
ST
FR

Lik
bo

LIMERICK PARKING SIGNS CHANGED TO READ 'RED LIGHT DISTRICT'

MAN RAMS GARDA SQUAD CAR WITH HORSE AND CART

WOMAN 'RANG 999 TO COMPLAIN ABOUT CHIPS'

Sex toys used at St Patrick's Day fundraiser

PARKI
RAIDE
PAY FO